NEED to KNOW

HIGHER MODERN STUDIES

Key facts at your fingertips

Paul Cr...

D1334113

HODDER
GIBSON
AN HACHETTE UK COMPANY

Every effort has been made to trace all copyright holders, but if any have been inadvertently overlooked, the Publishers will be pleased to make the necessary arrangements at the first opportunity.

Although every effort has been made to ensure that website addresses are correct at time of going to press, Hodder Education cannot be held responsible for the content of any website mentioned in this book. It is sometimes possible to find a relocated web page by typing in the address of the home page for a website in the URL window of your browser.

Orders: please contact Bookpoint Ltd, 130 Park Drive, Milton Park, Abingdon, Oxon OX14 4SE. Telephone: (44) 01235 827827. Fax: (44) 01235 400401. Email: education@bookpoint.co.uk. Lines are open from 9 a.m. to 5 p.m., Monday to Saturday, with a 24-hour message answering service. You can also order through our website: www.hoddereducation.co.uk. Hodder Gibson can also be contacted directly at hoddergibson@hodder.co.uk.

© Paul Creaney 2019

First published in 2019 by
Hodder Gibson, an imprint of Hodder Education,
An Hachette UK Company
211 Vincent Street
Glasgow G2 5QY

Impression number 10 9 8 7 6 5 4 3 2 1

Year 2023 2022 2021 2020 2019

All rights reserved. Apart from any use permitted under UK copyright law, no part of this publication may be reproduced or transmitted in any form or by any means, electronic or mechanical, including photocopying and recording, or held within any information storage and retrieval system, without permission in writing from the publisher or under licence from the Copyright Licensing Agency Limited. Further details of such licences (for reprographic reproduction) may be obtained from the Copyright Licensing Agency Limited, www.cla.co.uk.

Typeset by Aptara Inc., India
Printed in Spain

A catalogue record for this title is available from the British Library.

ISBN: 978 1 5104 5117 9

Hachette UK's policy is to use papers that are natural, renewable and recyclable products and made from wood grown in well-managed forests and other controlled sources. The logging and manufacturing processes are expected to conform to the environmental regulations of the country of origin.

Contents

Getting the most from this book

This *Need to Know* guide is designed to help you throughout your course as a companion to your learning and a revision aid in the months or weeks leading up to the final exams.

The following features in each section will help you get the most from the book.

You need to know

Each topic begins with a list summarising what you 'need to know' in this topic for the exam.

Exam tips

Key knowledge you need to demonstrate in the exam, tips on exam technique, common misconceptions to avoid and important things to remember.

Key terms

Definitions of **highlighted** terms in the text to make sure you know the essential terminology for your subject.

Do you know?

Questions at the end of each topic to test you on some of its key points. Check your answers here: **hoddereducation.co.uk/ needtoknow/answers**

Synoptic links

Reminders of how knowledge and skills from different topics in your Higher course relate to one another.

End of section questions

Questions at the end of each main section of the book to test your knowledge of the specification area covered. Check your answers here: **hoddereducation.co.uk/needtoknow/answers**

① Democracy in Scotland and the UK

1.1 Governance of Scotland

> **You need to know**
> - what democracy means
> - about the possible alternatives for the governance of Scotland, including pre-devolution arrangements, devo max, fiscal responsibility, a fully federalised system and/or independence

A **democracy** is a system of government by the whole population or all eligible members of a state, typically through elected representatives.

Extensions of devolved powers

Devo max

- **Devo max** or maximum devolution would allow the Scottish Parliament power over most reserved matters, except defence and foreign affairs.
- **Fiscal responsibility**:
  - ☐ Devolution of *all* tax and spending decisions would go to Scotland.
  - ☐ Scotland would be responsible for raising the money to fund its own spending through its own tax-raising.
  - ☐ The Scottish Government would be responsible for balancing its budget.
  - ☐ Fiscal responsibility would mean that the Scottish Government would have to set up a Scottish treasury and its own inland revenue system in order to collect taxes and pay for the services still reserved and provided by the UK Government (for example, defence and foreign affairs).

A fully federalised system

- Each country of the UK (Scotland, Wales, Northern Ireland and England) would have more powers and responsibility for its own affairs.
- Each country would remain part of the UK without breaking up the union.

> **Key term**
>
> Democracy 'Rule by the people'; the idea that the people should have a say and be able to influence what happens and what is decided.

> **Exam tip**
>
> Make sure you are able to distinguish between devo max, fiscal responsibility and a fully federalised system, because they are alternative extensions of devolved powers.

■ Note that at the moment, there is controversy around the fact that Scottish MPs can vote in Westminster on reserved matters but English MPs cannot vote on devolved matters. This means Scottish MPs could influence controversial votes in Westminster even though the matter would not affect their constituents.

Independence

■ Scotland would become an independent country and no longer be a part of the UK.
■ Scotland would govern itself with full control of its own affairs without interference from the UK.

The devolved settlement implemented in 1999

■ The Scotland Act defines the powers devolved to Scotland and those reserved by the UK Government.
■ Areas of dispute and conflict between the Scottish and UK Governments include:
  □ calls for additional power
  □ policy differences
  □ unclear areas of responsibilities
  Examples include student tuition fees and paying for elderly care.

Devolved and reserved powers

■ The Scottish Parliament has the power to introduce new laws on many issues. These are known as **devolved matters**.
■ The UK Parliament has retained the responsibility for other issues. These are known as **reserved matters**.

Devolved powers (Scottish Government)	Reserved powers (UK Government)
Agriculture, forestry and fisheries	Benefits and social security
Education and training	Broadcasting
Environment	Constitution
Health and social services	Defence
Housing	Employment
Law and order	Equal opportunities
Local government	Foreign policy
Sport and the arts	Immigration
Some forms of taxation	Trade and industry
Many forms of transport	

Exam tip

In the exam, you must be able to describe the alternatives for the governance of Scotland and analyse/evaluate the arguments for and against them.

Do you know?

1 What are the possible alternatives for the governance of Scotland?
2 What is meant by 'devolved powers'?
3 What is meant by 'reserved powers'?
4 What are the areas of dispute and conflict between the Scottish and UK Governments?

1.2 The UK's decision to leave the EU

You need to know

■ to what extent leaving the European Union will have positive implications for the UK
■ how to analyse the potential impact of leaving the European Union

Voting patterns in the 2016 EU referendum

Exam tip

In answering exam questions regarding the impact of Brexit, you can refer to issues affecting Scotland **or** the UK **or** both in your response.

Voted to leave	Voted to remain
UK (51.9%)	Scotland (62%)
England (53.4%)	Northern Ireland (55.8%)
Wales (52.5%)	

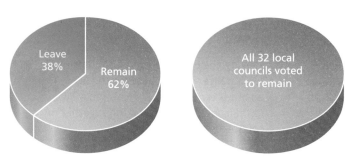

Figure 1.1 How Scotland voted in the 2016 EU referendum

Areas of dispute between Brexiteers and Remainers

The following table summarises some of the different views between Brexiteers and Remainers.

Key terms

Brexiteer Someone who wants the UK to leave the EU.

Remainer Someone who wants the UK to remain a part of the EU.

Issue	Brexiteer view	Remainer view
Membership fee	Leaving the EU would result in an immediate cost saving, as the country would no longer contribute to the EU budget	The UK has pledged to keep paying billions of pounds into the EU budget for years to come
Trade	The UK would be free to establish its own trade agreements	Outside the EU, the UK would lose tariff-free trade with its neighbours and reduce its negotiating power with the rest of the world
Investment	Investment will continue unaffected because Britain has a large trade deficit with the EU. It is in Europe's interest to find a compromise and so a deal to allow continued tariff-free trading will be secured even if the UK leaves the single market	The UK's attraction to investors and its status as one of the world's biggest financial centres would be diminished if it was no longer seen as a gateway to the EU for the likes of US banks. Also, financial firms based in the UK would lose the right to tariff-free trading across the EU
Sovereignty	EU institutions have taken sovereign power from the UK Parliament Leaving the EU will allow the UK to re-establish itself as a truly independent nation with connections to the rest of the world	EU membership involves a beneficial trade of sovereignty for influence, e.g. in return for agreeing to abide by EU rules, the UK has a seat around the negotiating table and a louder voice on the world stage UK sovereignty is not secured out of the EU, in fact the UK Government will still be bound by membership of NATO, the UN, the WTO and various treaties and agreements with other nations but will be giving up its influence in Europe
Immigration	Immigration should be cut and Britain should take control of its borders	While current immigration has led to some difficulties with housing and service provision, the net effect has been positive
Jobs	Less immigration will mean more jobs for the people who remain	Many jobs will be lost and trade and investment will fall
Security	The UK's defences will become severely weakened by staying in because the open border does not allow Britain to check and control people, making it harder to prevent terrorist attacks	Leaving the EU will be seriously detrimental for Britain's security because the EU was an important part of Britain's security, exchanging data and working together on counterterrorism

Key terms

Sovereignty The power and authority of a state to govern itself.

NATO North Atlantic Treaty Organization.

WTO World Trade Organization.

Theresa May's Brexit deal

- Brexiteers argue that the prime minister's current deal binds the UK too closely to the EU.
- Remainers argue that it creates obstacles and barriers to trade and threatens future relationships.
- Both Brexiteers and Remainers oppose a 'backstop' agreement because it would treat countries within the UK differently, keeping the UK within a customs union to ensure an open border between the Republic of Ireland (a member of the EU) and Northern Ireland (a part of the UK).

Brexit alternatives

Norway-plus deal with the EU

- This would be similar to what currently happens in Norway, which is not an EU member but is part of the European Economic Area.
- This model would allow the UK to remain a part of the single market, with goods, services and people continuing to move within freely and reducing perceived disruptions to the economy.

Canada-style trade arrangement

- This arrangement is similar to the model in Canada.
- It would mean access to, but not membership of, the single market.

Summary

- Brexiteers argue it would be in the interests of other European countries to re-establish free trade with the UK.
- Remainers argue that the EU will want to make life hard for Britain in order to discourage other countries from wanting to leave, so the UK will be forced to compromise on any deal.

Do you know?

1 Which countries voted to leave and which voted to remain in the 2016 EU referendum?
2 How did Scotland vote in the 2016 EU referendum?
3 List three areas of dispute between Brexiteers and Remainers.
4 What are two alternatives to Brexit?

1.3 Holding government to account

You need to know
■ how to evaluate the effectiveness of parliament in holding the government to account

Holding government to account

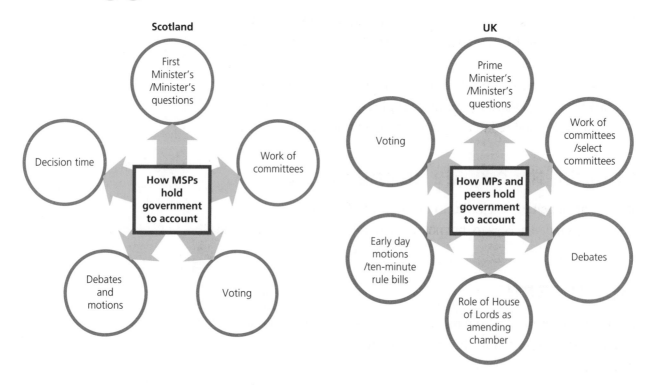

Influences on effectiveness

The following can impact on the effectiveness of parliament in holding the government to account:

■ type of government: minority, majority or coalition
■ size of government (majority/minority)
■ party and backbench loyalty
■ whip system

Methods and their effectiveness

Method	Effective because ...	Ineffective because ...
Questions	Answers must be given Forces PM/FM and ministers to be accountable	MPs and MSPs can be reluctant to criticise own party members
Committees Westminster and Scottish Parliament committees Westminster select committees work in both houses and scrutinise government policy Scottish Parliament committees scrutinise the work of the Scottish government	The House of Commons has departmental select committees that 'shadow' government departments They expose inadequacies and can influence policies and effectively criticise government The executive cannot influence membership of select committees and chairs are chosen by backbench MPs Chairs are paid an extra salary, allowing them to be more independent Committees often agree across party divisions and frequently produce critical reports Committees have the power to question ministers on all aspects of the policies of the government. Ministers must answer the questions asked	Party loyalty Amendments proposed by committees are rarely accepted Committees have few resources and little time to be effective Select committees cannot enforce their recommendations and have no control over legislation
Relationship and balance of power between legislative and executive bodies	Fusion of powers Size of majority Strength of opposition PM or FM popularity	'Majority government' means the majority of MPs and MSPs belong to the governing party and are more likely to support rather than to criticise
Public petition system and evidence taking in the Scottish Parliament	The public can influence the work and legislation of the Scottish Parliament through the public petition system and evidence taking	Most petitioners are older, well-off, white men with a degree, which is not reflective of the general public

Key terms

Committee Small group of representatives from different parties who consider specific issues and report back to the government with recommendations.

Scrutinise Examine closely.

Backbench MP Any MP or member of the House of Lords who is not a government MP or shadow government MP. In the House of Commons, backbench MPs sit in the benches at the back and behind their party's spokespeople (who are called frontbenchers).

Exam tip

Parliamentary representatives include MPs, peers and MSPs. In the exam you can refer to representatives in either Scotland **or** the UK **or** both Scotland **and** the UK.

Importance of committees to the democratic process

- Parliamentary select committees are important to the democratic process because of their ability to call high-profile witnesses to committee hearings.

- This is vital as it allows MPs and peers to hold government ministers and officials to account, as well as gathering evidence from experts and stakeholders outside government.
- Select committees are important to the democratic process because they can:
  - hold elected representatives, public officials and business people to account. For example, Greg Dyke (the director-general of the BBC) and Rupert Murdoch (the owner of News International) have appeared before committees.
  - provide legitimacy. Since hearings are conducted in a public forum, government ministers who appear before a select committee are able to account for their actions in this public forum and government is therefore seen as more open and democratic.
  - expose evidence. Because committees can gain access to people, documents and records along with statements and testimonies, it is very difficult to conceal information.
  - raise the profile of issues. Since the work of committees is routinely reported in the media, their role is seen as increasingly important to the democratic process.
  - allow involvement and participation of the general public. The general public can get involved and participate by having their voice heard in advance of an inquiry through each committee's online forum.
  - allow the formation of democratic political consensus. The findings of a committee can result in cross-party attempts to introduce legislation.
  - change government policy. It is estimated that approximately 40 per cent of committee recommendations are accepted by government, thereby increasing the democratic process.

Table 1.1 Examples of UK Government committees

Committee	Effective because ...	Ineffective because ...
Public Accounts Committee	Chaired by a member of the opposition Examines all government expenditure High level of independence	Cannot enforce its recommendations
Liaison Committee	Contains all the key committee chairs Calls the prime minister to account	Only meets twice a year

Scottish Parliament committees that scrutinise the work of the Scottish Government are of similar importance to the democratic process. They can:
- scrutinise the work of the Scottish Government
- consider and comment on legislative proposals

- conduct inquiries and publish reports
- introduce committee bills

Table 1.2 Examples of Scottish Parliament committees

Scottish Parliament committees	
Mandatory committees	■ Equal Opportunities ■ European and External Relations ■ Finance ■ Public Audit ■ Public Petitions ■ Standards, Procedures and Public Appointments ■ Subordinate Legislation
Subject committees	■ Economy, Energy and Tourism ■ Education and Culture ■ Health and Sport ■ Infrastructure and Capital Investment ■ Justice ■ Local Government and Regeneration ■ Rural Affairs, Climate Change and Environment
Ad hoc committees	■ Issues and legislation

Stages of a bill in the Scottish Parliament

Stage 1
- Parliamentary committees consider the general principles of the **bill** and ask the general public for their input
- Parliament debates and reaches a decision on the general principles of the bill

↓

Stage 2
- A committee considers the bill in more detail and considers amendments if required

↓

Stage 3
- Further amendments are considered before parliament decides whether to pass or reject the bill

↓

Royal assent
- If parliament passes the bill, it needs **royal assent** to become part of Scottish law as an act of the Scottish Parliament

Key terms

Bill A proposal for a new law, or a proposal to change an existing law, presented for debate before parliament.

Royal assent Approval from the monarch.

Stages of a bill in Westminster

- In Westminster, a bill can start in the House of Commons or the House of Lords.
- It must be approved in the same form by both houses before becoming law.

Bill starting in the House of Commons

House of Commons
First reading
Second reading
Committee stage
Report stage
Third reading

↓

House of Lords
First reading
Second reading
Committee stage
Report stage
Third reading

↓

Consideration of amendments

↓

Royal assent

Bill starting in the House of Lords

House of Lords
First reading
Second reading
Committee stage
Report stage
Third reading

↓

House of Commons
First reading
Second reading
Committee stage
Report stage
Third reading

↓

Consideration of amendments

↓

Royal assent

Do you know?

1 Who are parliamentary representatives?
2 Give two ways MSPs and two ways MPs can hold the government to account.
3 What can Scottish Parliament committees do?
4 What are the stages of a bill in the Scottish Parliament?
5 What are the stages of a bill in the UK Parliament?

1.4 Electoral systems used in the UK

You need to know

- how to evaluate the effectiveness of one voting system you have studied in providing fair representation
- how to analyse the ways in which an electoral system you have studied allows accurate representation of the electorate's views

Exam tip

When answering exam questions that evaluate the effectiveness of voting systems and analyse electoral systems, you can refer to Scotland **or** the UK **or** both in your answer.

First Past the Post

- The First Past the Post (FPTP) electoral system is used in UK general elections.
- There is one candidate per party on the ballot paper so if voters support the party but don't like the candidate, they have to choose their disliked candidate or vote for a party that they don't support.
- In 2010, the Conservatives won with a minority so formed a coalition government with the Liberal Democrats.
- In 2015:
  - □ In Scotland, the SNP won 95 per cent of the seats (56 of the 59 available) with 50 per cent of the vote: this was a greatly disproportionate result.
  - □ In England, the UK Independence Party (UKIP) won over 14 per cent of the votes, but won only one seat (that it had previously held).
  - □ The Liberal Democrats' share of the vote dropped from 23.5 per cent in 2010 to only 8 per cent, and their seats dropped from 57 to only 8, which were spread across many regions of the country.
  - □ The Conservatives won with a majority of 37 per cent of the vote but held 51 per cent of the seats.
  - □ The Belfast South candidate won with 24.5 per cent of the vote, so three-quarters of voters in the constituency did not want the MP they got.
- In 2017:
  - □ After the EU referendum in 2016, the UKIP leader Nigel Farage resigned and within a year support for UKIP collapsed (due to a feeling of having achieved its aim and because it lacked leadership).
  - □ The Liberal Democrats' share of the vote fell by another 0.5 per cent from its 2015 level but their seats increased slightly from 8 to 12.
  - □ The Conservatives increased their UK share of the vote to over 42 per cent, an increase of around 6 per cent from 2015, winning more seats than any other party, but in England they lost seats and were left without a majority.
  - □ The Conservatives did gain seats in Scotland, at the expense of the SNP whose 2015 gains evaporated. This left the Conservatives relying on a 'confidence and supply' arrangement with the Democratic Unionist Party (DUP), in order to hold on to power.

Key term

(First Past the Post) FPTP The electoral system used in UK general elections to elect MPs to the House of Commons in the Westminster Parliament.

- ☐ The Conservatives won 318 seats out of the 650 available (a minority, less than half) but, with the support of the DUP (who won ten seats), together they had a majority of 328 seats.
- ☐ The biggest winner was the Labour Party, whose share of the vote increased to 40 per cent from just over 30 per cent in 2015. However, they only got 262 seats – that is, 2 per cent fewer votes than the Conservatives but 56 fewer seats.
- ☐ In Scotland, the SNP's almost total dominance in 2015 lasted only 2 years, and multi-party politics then resumed. Support for the SNP reduced significantly from 50 per cent to just below 37 per cent, and FPTP led to a radical reduction of its seats in the Westminster Parliament from 59 to 35.

> **Key term**
>
> **BME** Stands for 'black and minority ethnic'.

Strengths of FPTP	Weaknesses of FPTP
- Simple/easy for people to cast a vote (just mark one 'X' against your preferred candidate) - Votes are counted quickly and easily, and voters can easily understand how the result happened - Provides a strong majority government (usually) - Provides a strong/stable single-party government (usually) - Provides strong constituency links - Blocks extremist parties - By-elections allow constituents to always choose who their MP is if the seat becomes vacant between general elections - Turnout levels in the twenty-first century are lower than those for the twentieth century. However, in 2015, 30.7 million people voted in the election and 39.3 million voted in 2017 - The proportion of MPs with local majority support has increased across the last three general elections, reaching a high of 72% in 2017 - The proportion of voters positively supporting the governing Conservatives in 2017 was 29.2%, an increase on the levels opposite	- Reduces choice - Leads to a two-party system; smaller parties have difficulty winning seats due to the spread of support - Disproportionality: the number of MPs a party gains is not in proportion to the number of votes the party got - Does not always produce a strong/stable single-party government - Constituencies can be won with a minority of votes; large minorities of voters regard the seats awarded to the largest parties and the lack of seats for smaller parties as illegitimate and distorted - Votes are not of equal value - Produces many wasted votes - FPTP discriminates against smaller parties with a spread of national support which usually come second or third in many constituencies, e.g. the Liberal Democrats (plus UKIP in 2010 and 2015), who get millions of votes but few or no MPs - The proportion of MPs with local majority support in their seats fell between 1974 and 2005 (when it reached just 55%) - Single-party governments are based on small minorities of voters (35–42% between 2001 and 2017), and even smaller proportions of positively supporting voters (22–24% between 2001 and 2015) - The proportion of MPs in Westminster who are holding seats not justified by their share of the votes was above a fifth between 1997 and 2015. - Westminster has only tiny proportions of people from manual working-class backgrounds and from **BME** minorities - Gender representation remains overwhelmingly male, with female MPs forming 20–29% of the total for the last two decades. In 2017, female MPs made up 32% of the Commons, but this is still far short of the 50/50 goal

Additional Member System

- The **Additional Member System (AMS)** is the electoral system used in Scottish Parliament elections.
- The first two Scottish Parliament elections (1999 and 2003) led to coalition governments between the Labour and the Liberal Democrat parties.
- In 2007, the SNP formed a minority government. This meant they had difficulty fulfilling their manifesto promises and getting legislation passed as they had to seek support from opposition parties (mostly the Green Party) on what was termed a policy-by-policy basis.
- In 2011, the SNP were able to form a majority government. This meant they could drive forward with their manifesto and pass legislation more easily. As a result they initiated a Scottish independence referendum.
- In 2016, the SNP again won the election but, as in 2007, with a minority and again sought opposition support on a policy-by-policy basis.
- One result of AMS is that smaller parties such as the Greens and the Scottish Socialist Party have achieved seats along with some independents, increasing the influence of the backbench.

Strengths of AMS	Weaknesses of AMS
- Allows proportionality - Provides strong constituency links - Produces a **coalition government** (usually) - Favours minority parties - Provides more choice - Reduces wasted votes	- Complicated system/not as easy to understand - Produces a coalition government (usually) - Gives minority parties more power - Can produce an unstable/weak government - Party lists: the parties decide who is on the party list and so Party List MSPs are not elected directly by the public - Two MSP types: Constituency MSPs and Party List MSPs - No by-elections: the parties can place an MSP into a vacant seat without the public having a say

Key terms

AMS (Additional Member System) The electoral system used to elect MSPs to the Scottish Parliament.

Coalition government A government formed by more than one political party. Parties may decide to form a coalition government where no single party has a clear working majority in parliament following an election.

STV (Single Transferrable Vote) The electoral system used in Scotland to elect councillors to local government.

Single Transferable Vote

- The **Single Transferable Vote (STV)** electoral system is used in Scottish local government elections.
- In 2017, in the Scottish council elections, 29 of the 32 council areas had no single party with overall control. Three were controlled by independent candidates, 18 were coalitions and 11 were controlled by a minority.

Strengths of STV	Weaknesses of STV
▪ Allows proportionality ▪ Favours minority parties ▪ Votes cast are of equal value ▪ Reduces wasted votes ▪ Increased choice as voters can choose candidates from different parties or independent candidates	▪ Confusing system/not as easy to understand ▪ Produces multi-member wards ▪ No direct councillor/voter link ▪ Gives more power to smaller parties

Comparison of UK electoral systems

	Representation	Choice	Fair	Complex
FPTP	Strong constituency links Single-member constituencies	Limited choice	Not fair	No Fewer spoilt ballot papers
AMS	Some constituency links Small single-member and larger regional constituencies	More choice	More fair	Yes More spoilt ballot papers
STV	No constituency links Multi-member wards	Most choice	Most fair	Yes Most spoilt ballot papers

■ The UK held two general elections quite close together:
  ☐ one in 2015 (at the end of 5 years of a coalition government)
  ☐ another in 2017 (a snap election called by Prime Minister Theresa May)
■ They were important because they led to some alterations in how FPTP operates, reflecting changes in the party system.

Do you know?

1 What electoral systems are used in elections within the UK?
2 Which electoral system is considered to be most fair?
3 Which electoral system is considered to offer most choice?
4 What is a coalition government?

Exam tip

You must be able to evaluate these voting systems in terms of representation, choice, fairness and complexity.

Exam tips

■ You must also be able to evaluate the impact of voting systems on election results at local, devolved or UK levels.

■ You must be able to describe and analyse any possible outcomes of elections, including majority or minority administration, and coalition.

1.5 Factors that influence voting behaviour

You need to know

- to what extent age is the most influential factor on voting behaviour
- how to analyse the influence of the media on voting behaviour
- to what extent some factors are more important than others in influencing voting behaviour

Class and voting behaviour

Table 1.3 **Descriptions of social classes**

Social class	Description	Occupation
AB	Upper class – elite	Higher and intermediate managerial, administrative, professional occupations
C1	Upper-middle class	Supervisory, clerical and junior managerial, administrative, professional occupations
C2	Lower-middle class	Skilled manual occupations
DE	Working class	Semi-skilled and unskilled manual occupations, unemployed and lowest grade occupations

Table 1.4 **Voting by class for the two main parties in UK general elections (majority) (Conservative = blue; Labour = red)**

Class	1979	1992	1997	2010	2015	2017
AB						
C1						
C2					No difference	
DE						

- 'Alignment' is where the electorate vote in groups either by their social class or age, aligning themselves with a particular party and always voting for that party.
- In recent elections there has been evidence of dealignment occurring.

> ### Exam tip
>
> To answer questions in the exam regarding voting behaviour, you can refer to Scotland **or** the UK **or** both in your response.

> ### Key term
>
> **Social class** Economic groups that people are assigned to based on their earnings.

■ Figure 1.2 shows that:
- ☐ a majority of voters who earned less than £20,000 were in favour of independence (53 per cent)
- ☐ there was very little difference between 'yes' and 'no' voters among those earning above £30,000
- ☐ in terms of class, those earning between £20,000 and £30,000 had the biggest impact on the outcome of the referendum, voting 'no' by a difference of 57 per cent to 44 per cent

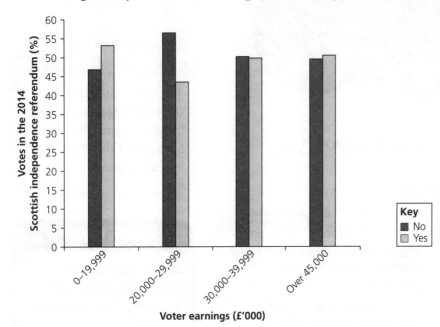

Figure 1.2 Voting by class (earnings) in the 2014 Scottish independence referendum

■ **Note**: 65 per cent of those living in one of the 20 per cent most deprived neighbourhoods in Scotland voted 'yes', compared with just 36 per cent of those in the 20 per cent most affluent neighbourhoods.

Age and voting behaviour

Table 1.5 Voting by age for the two main parties in UK general elections (majority) (Conservative = blue; Labour = red)

Age	1979	1992	1997	2010	2015	2017
18–24						
25–34						
35–44					No difference	
45–54						
55–64						
65+						

> ## Exam tip
>
> It would be helpful for the exam to revise examples of how voters of different classes and ages voted in recent elections and referenda. (See the example of the 2014 Scottish independence referendum and remember that class is related to earnings.)

- Looking at Table 1.5, it is clear that:
  - □ since 2015, young voters are more likely to vote Labour
  - □ since 2015, older voters are more likely to vote Conservative
  - □ in 2017, those aged 18–24, including first-time voters, voted for Labour and Jeremy Corbyn
  - □ in 2017, those over 45 voted Conservative
- When Labour won many university town and inner-city seats in 2017 (helped by young voters), the media referred to a 'youthquake' in terms of young people re-participating in voting.
- Turnout among young people was greater in 2017 and they voted in line with most social groups.
- It is estimated that for every 10 years a person ages, they are 9 per cent more likely to vote Conservative.
- Figure 1.3 shows that in the 2014 Scottish independence referendum:
  - □ older voters were strongly in favour of Scotland remaining part of the UK, with around 2 in 3 people over the age of 70 voting 'no'
  - □ most 16–17 year olds, who were eligible to vote, voted 'no'
  - □ most young voters aged between 16 and 24 also voted 'no'
  - □ 54 per cent of teenagers and those in their early twenties voted 'no' to independence, supporting the Union
  - □ those aged 25–29 were in the age group most likely to vote 'yes', with 62 per cent voting for independence

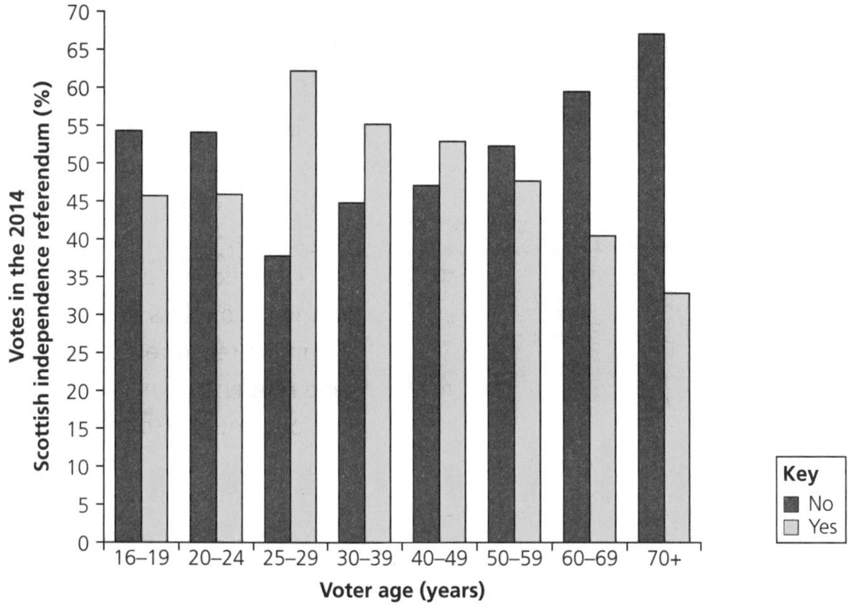

Figure 1.3 Voting by age in the 2014 Scottish independence referendum

The 2017 EU referendum

- Most 'remain' votes were cast by those who were young, middle class, had received more education and/or were BME voters.
- Most 'leave' votes were cast by those who were older, working class, had received less education and/or were white voters.
- A majority of 18–34 year olds in every social class voted to remain, while a majority of those aged 55+ in every class voted to leave.
- Within every age group a majority of AB voters voted to remain, and a majority of CD voters voted to leave.
- Within each class a majority of younger people voted to remain, and a majority of older people voted to leave.
- The main difference was among those aged 35–54, where the majority of AB voters chose 'remain' while the majority of CD voters chose 'leave'.

The media and voting behaviour

Table 1.6 **Newspaper readership at the time of the 2017 UK general election (% of votes by newspaper readers)**

Newspaper	Conservative (%)	Labour (%)
Telegraph	79	12
Daily Express	77	15
Daily Mail	74	17
Sun	59	30
The Times	58	24
Financial Times	40	39
Daily Star	38	49
Daily Mirror	19	68
Independent	15	66
Guardian	8	73

- Looking at Table 1.6, we see that in the 2017 UK general election:
  - □ voters tended to vote in line with the party allegiances of their preferred newspapers
  - □ most readers of the *Daily Mail*, the *Telegraph*, the *Daily Express*, the *Sun* and *The Times* voted Conservative
  - □ most readers of the *Guardian*, the *Daily Mirror,* the *Daily Star* and the *Independent* voted Labour
  - □ the *Financial Times* had the most divided readership

Exam tip

You must be prepared to mention factors other than the one given in the question in your response, such as:
- gender, region and religion
- targeted political advertising
- 'fake news'

Exam tips

- If you are asked about the extent to which class or age is the most influential factor on voting behaviour, you should analyse and evaluate the influence of class or age on voting in recent elections and referenda.
- You should also mention factors other than class or age that influence voting behaviour like the media, gender, geographical location or residence, ethnicity, party leader competence, image and issues.

Do you know?

1 What are the three main influences on voting behaviour in the UK?

2 Which social class tends to vote Conservative and which votes Labour?

3 In the 2017 UK general election, which party did most young people vote for?

4 Which UK newspaper readers were most likely to vote Conservative and which were most likely to vote Labour in the 2017 UK general election?

1.6 Influencing government decision making

You need to know

- how to analyse the ways in which individuals and groups in society can influence government decision making
- how to discuss the ways citizens participate in the political process

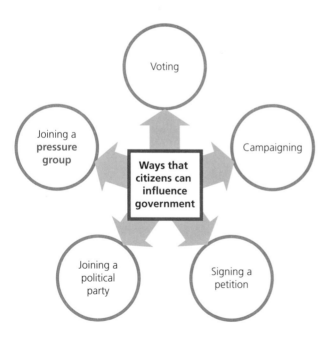

Voting

Joining a pressure group

Ways that citizens can influence government

Campaigning

Joining a political party

Signing a petition

Key term

Pressure group A group of like-minded people who put pressure on the government and decision-makers in an attempt to achieve their aims.

Pressure groups

Types of pressure group

- **Cause groups** campaign and lobby for specific causes on behalf of others, for example, the Child Poverty Action Group (CPAG). The Scottish Free School Meals Campaign, led by CPAG in Scotland, put pressure on the Scottish Government to announce that all children in Primary 1, 2 and 3 in Scotland are entitled to a healthy, free school lunch.
- **Interest groups** campaign and lobby for specific interests of their own, for example, the British Medical Association (BMA). The BMA lobbied the UK and Scottish governments, putting pressure on them to allow international graduates of UK medical schools to apply for jobs in Scotland on the same basis as other trainees.

Status of pressure groups

Insider pressure groups	Outsider pressure groups
<ul><li>Views are compatible with government</li><li>Advised and consulted by decision-makers</li><li>Work in partnership with decision-makers</li></ul>	<ul><li>Views are incompatible with government</li><li>Not consulted by decision-makers</li><li>Ignore decision-makers, so resort to taking direct action</li></ul>

Importance of pressure groups for democracy

Pressure groups enhance democracy by ...	Pressure groups detract from democracy by ...
<ul><li>increasing participation</li><li>including minority views</li><li>promoting discussion and debate</li></ul>	<ul><li>being undemocratic</li><li>promoting minority views</li><li>the 'tyranny' of the minority</li><li>using direct action/illegal methods</li><li>their lack of scrutiny and accountability</li></ul>

Pressure group methods

- Methods used by pressure groups can involve direct and/or indirect action.
- Examples of direct action include:
  - ☐ demonstrations
  - ☐ strikes
  - ☐ media/publicity campaigns/stunts
  - ☐ civil disobedience

Key terms

Cause group Campaigns for specific causes on behalf of others.

Interest group Campaigns for their own interests.

Exam tip

In answering exam questions on pressure groups, you can refer to individuals and groups in Scotland **or** the UK **or** both in your response.

Exam tip

You must demonstrate that you understand the difference between the insider and outsider status of pressure groups.

- Examples of indirect action include:
  - ☐ lobbying government ministers and civil servants
  - ☐ lobbying parliament (MPs/peers/MSPs) and committees
  - ☐ forming relationships with political parties, for example, through funding and donations
- Underpinning this are several factors that influence the success of any pressure group, namely:
  - ☐ its status and size
  - ☐ the amount of political support it receives
  - ☐ the resources available to it
  - ☐ its membership
  - ☐ its organisation and leadership
  - ☐ the finances available
  - ☐ public attitudes towards it
  - ☐ its views of government

The media

- The media is a form of mass communication either through broadcasting, publishing or the internet.
- Examples include newspapers, television/radio and social media like Facebook and Twitter.

Social media

- In the 2015 UK general election, campaigning parties spent a total of £1.3 million on Facebook.
- In 2017, this figure rose to £3.2 million, almost three times the 2015 value.
- The Conservatives spent the most in both elections:
  - ☐ In 2015, they spent £1.2 million on Facebook, resulting in a successful campaign for then Prime Minister David Cameron.
  - ☐ In 2017, they spent almost double that figure – £2.1 million on Facebook and £18.5 million in total on social media – but with less impact for Prime Minister Theresa May, as they lost their parliamentary majority.
- Labour lost badly in 2015 and increased online campaigning in 2017. The party spent just over £0.5 million on Facebook and £11 million in total on social media, improving its contact creator software to allow it to target named voters identified by its canvassing via Facebook.
- Both the Conservative and Labour parties used social media in different ways. The Conservatives focused on 'attack ads' while Labour's approach was more organic and positive.

Exam tip

To show analysis in the exam you need to know that, compared with broadcast media, online political messaging is far less regulated. Broadcasters are under strict political balance rules but this is not the same online. As a result, social media can happily be biased and one-sided, increasing their influence.

Conservative Party use of social media	Labour Party use of social media
■ The Conservatives' use of Facebook in 2015 was very effective ■ In 2017, the Conservative focus was for slick, paid-for 'attack ads' which were not as effective as expected ■ The Conservatives spent £18.5 million in total on social media but lost their government majority	■ The Labour Party did not use social media effectively in 2015 ■ In 2017, Labour's social media activity was much more organic and positive, and as a result was more effective than the Conservatives' ■ In terms of digital election campaigns, Labour seemed to do better than the Conservatives in 2017, with organic shares and outside groups overcoming the difference in cash spent by the Conservatives on Facebook advertising ■ Labour spent £11 million in total on social media (less than the Conservatives) and gained more MPs

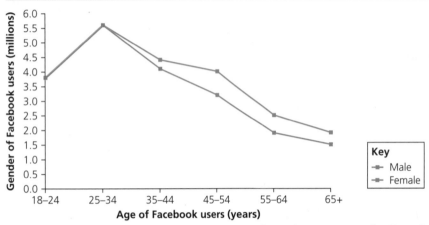

Figure 1.4 Facebook users in the UK by age (years) and gender (millions)

Newspapers and television

■ Many people form their opinions based on what they read in newspapers and watch on television.

■ This makes newspapers and broadcasters very influential.

■ By raising and highlighting issues and causes they ignite a fuel of publicity, attracting the support of the public who in turn can put pressure on the government and so influence the decision-making process.

■ The *Sun* is the most-read newspaper in the UK. It is also the most accessed by mobile device.

■ The *Guardian* is the most-accessed newspaper by desktop computer.

Table 1.7 Influence of the media on the 2015 and 2017 UK general elections

2015	2017
■ Television was the most effective media influence with 62% of voters being influenced ■ 61% of those were influenced by the televised party leaders' debate, 38% by national news, but only 16% by party political broadcasts ■ 11% of voters were influenced by social media (7% by Facebook and 4% by Twitter) ■ Newspapers were effective in influencing voters but far less than television ■ 25% of voters were influenced by newspapers, mostly the *Guardian* and *The Times* ■ 17% of voters were influenced by websites ■ 14% of voters were influenced by radio	■ The biggest social media election ever, but television and newspapers still influenced more voters than social media ■ 60% of voters were influenced by television ■ 45% of voters were influenced by newspapers (16% by the *Guardian* and 13% by the *Daily Mail*) ■ 15% of voters got political news from Facebook, 8% from Twitter and 4% from Buzzfeed ■ Digital media sources were more popular among 18–24 year olds, although even among this group traditional news sources remained the most popular sources of political news

Do you know?

1 State the ways in which citizens can influence government decision making.

2 Give three differences between the status of insider and outsider pressure groups.

3 Give three ways in which pressure groups enhance democracy and three ways in which they detract from democracy.

4 What has been the main form of social media used by political parties to influence voters?

End of section 1 questions

1 What is meant by 'devo max'?

2 What would the effect of full fiscal responsibility be for Scotland?

3 Outline the main devolved powers of the Scottish Government.

4 What are the arguments against Prime Minister Theresa May's Brexit deal?

5 Which groups were more likely to vote 'no' and 'yes' in the 2014 Scottish independence referendum?

6 Outline the factors that determine the effectiveness of parliamentary representatives in holding the government to account.

7 Outline the effectiveness of two UK Government committees in holding the government to account.

8 Why are committees important to the democratic process?

9 Outline the main stages in the passage of a bill in the Scottish Parliament **or** Westminster.

10 Outline the strengths and weaknesses of the electoral systems used in the UK.

11 Outline the impact that each of the electoral systems used in the UK had on the outcome of elections from 2010 to 2017.

12 Outline how class, age and the media have influenced voting behaviour in recent elections in the UK.

13 Other than class, age and the media, what other factors have influenced voting behaviour in recent elections in the UK?

14 Explain whether pressure groups enhance or detract from democracy in the UK.

15 Outline the effect of social media on UK elections.

16 Compare the influence of the media on the 2015 and 2017 UK general elections.

2 Social issues in the UK

Option 1 Social inequality

2.1 Income and wealth inequality

You need to know

■ the reasons why income and wealth inequality exist

Causes of income and wealth inequality

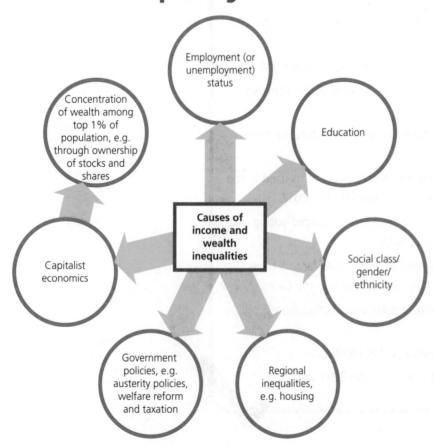

Exam tip

In the exam you can refer to relevant and contemporary reasons why income and wealth inequality exist in either Scotland **or** the UK, **or** both Scotland **and** the UK.

Exam tips

■ Income and wealth refer to economic issues. When answering these questions in the exam, you must describe the causes of economic inequality, giving balanced analytical/ evaluative comments, and explain why they exist.

■ The diagram shows some possible approaches but these are not compulsory and the list is not exhaustive.

Employment status

- One major cause of income inequality is linked to the ability to access well-paid employment.
- When unemployment is high, more people depend on welfare and benefits so inequality increases.
- However, many people who are in work still experience poverty.

In-work poverty	Over half (52%) of working-age adults in Scotland who are in poverty are from working households.
Causes of in-work poverty	■ Zero-hours contracts ■ Low pay ■ Part-time employment ■ Childcare costs
Unskilled work	There has been a decline in manufacturing and so less full-time manual work is available. Unskilled workers have experienced low wage growth, thus increasing income inequality.

Education

- Pupils from poorer households are less likely to achieve higher levels of education than those from richer households.
- They usually leave school earlier, have low job prospects and are more likely to earn lower wages, leading to income and wealth inequality.

Gender/ethnicity

- Over their working lives, most women work for a shorter time in paid employment than men, resulting in lower pensions.
- Consequently, women are more than one-and-a-half times more likely to live in poverty during their retirement than men.
- Women and those from BME groups can experience discrimination in the job market:
  - ☐ They can find it more difficult to get employment.
  - ☐ When they do, they usually only hold part-time/low-paid work with fewer opportunities for promotion to higher-paying roles.
- In Scotland, people from BME groups are four times more likely to live in overcrowded housing and twice as likely to be unemployed and poor.

Regional inequalities

- Income inequality is linked to where you live and work.
- The same job in one city can pay more than in another city or in a rural area.
- Edinburgh and London have higher average salaries than other smaller cities and towns.
- This leads to regional income and wealth inequality.

Accommodation costs

- The high cost of renting accommodation makes it more difficult for young people and those on a low income to save and accumulate wealth.
- This can also prevent people from moving between regions in search of work.
- First-time home buyers find it difficult to get onto the housing ladder due to the large deposits required.
- Thus, the cost associated with owning or even renting accommodation can add to wealth inequality.

Government policies

- The government exercises direct and indirect taxes in the UK:
  - ☐ Direct taxes include income tax, which is calculated based on the earnings or profit an individual makes.
  - ☐ Indirect taxes include taxes on goods and services bought by individuals, such as those below.

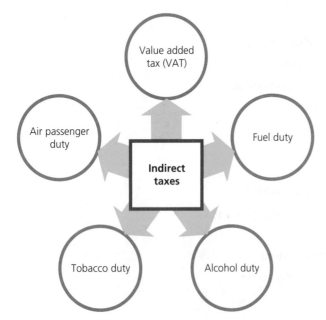

- Indirect taxes can cause wealth inequality because the poor pay a higher proportion of their income on indirect taxation than the rich.
- Government progressive or regressive tax policies can also cause income and wealth inequality.

Progressive tax policy	Regressive tax policy
■ The richest proportionally pay more tax ■ The poorest proportionally pay less tax	■ Proportionally more tax is taken from people on lower incomes ■ Proportionally less tax is taken from high earners
Result: income inequality tends to fall	Result: income inequality tends to rise

Do you know?

1 List the main causes of income and wealth inequality.

2 What are the main causes of in-work poverty?

3 What is the effect of a regressive tax system on income inequality?

4 Give three examples of indirect taxation.

2.2 Health inequality

You need to know

- ■ the reasons why health inequality exists
- ■ the role of poverty as a cause of poor health
- ■ the role of lifestyle choices on health

- The reasons why health inequality exists are complex and widespread.
- While poverty is a major reason why health inequality exists, age, gender, the lifestyle choices people make and ethnicity are also important factors.

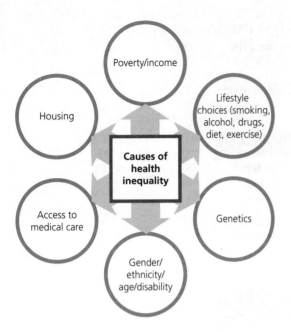

Exam tip

The diagram shows some possible approaches but these are not compulsory and the list is not exhaustive.

Causes of health inequality

Poverty

- People living in poverty are more likely to:
  - ☐ have less healthy diets
  - ☐ live in poor-quality housing
  - ☐ be unable to afford to adequately heat their homes
  - ☐ live in more deprived areas
  - ☐ have difficulty accessing adequate health services
  - ☐ have mental health issues (e.g. stress and high blood pressure from relying on welfare and worrying about money)

Lifestyle choices

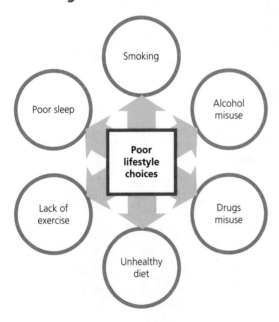

- Fundamentally, bad lifestyle choices result in bad health, while good lifestyle choices result in good health.
- Choosing to smoke, drink alcohol, take drugs, eat a diet high in salt and fat (which includes more junk food) and avoid exercise all contributes negatively to a person's health.
- Poorer households are more likely to experience higher levels of smoking, alcohol and drug misuse and less healthy diets than the rich, leading to inequalities in health between the poor and rich.
- While there has been a fall in children smoking in Scotland, 34 per cent of adults in the most deprived areas smoke compared to 9 per cent in the least deprived areas.

Genetics

- Hereditary health issues are another reason why health inequalities exist.
- A person's genetics or hereditary factors can cause health issues, for example, heart problems.
- Health inequalities can exist between those with a healthy family history and those with an unhealthy one.
- While this is generally outside an individual's control, it can also be linked to other factors such as their lifestyle choices and where they live, over which they do have some control.
- Nevertheless, scientists say that there is a 'skinny' gene that helps some people stay thin. Researchers found that slim people have fewer genes linked to obesity and changes in gene regions that are now linked with being healthily slim.

Gender

- There are inequalities in **morbidity** and **mortality rates** between men and women.
- Women tend to live longer than men but report more health problems.
- In affluent areas, men can have 23.8 more years of good health and women 22.6 years compared to the most deprived areas.

Key term

Morbidity rate The rate of disease in a country.

Mortality rate The rate of death in a country.

Ethnicity

- In the UK, BME groups experience poorer health than white people, however, there are also differences between BME groups.
- The main reason for ethnic health inequality is related to poverty. BME groups are more likely than white people to:
  - ☐ experience lower income levels
  - ☐ have a higher dependence on welfare

- ☐ have higher unemployment levels
- ☐ live in deprived areas
- However, other factors like the impact of migration, racism, discrimination and certain genetic problems can also affect their health.

Age

- Children born into poor families are more likely to have worse health than those born into rich families.
- They are especially likely to experience poor nutrition, chronic disease and mental health problems.
- Young people employed on zero-hours contracts are more likely to have worse mental and physical health than young people with the stability of full-time employment.

Housing

- Housing causes health inequality between rich and poor because of the effects of:
  - ☐ housing costs
  - ☐ housing quality
  - ☐ fuel poverty
- Many people cannot afford to live in a home that is warm and dry and have to decide to 'heat or eat', and this can lead to health problems.

Synoptic link

Inequalities in health are related to poverty, which is linked to inequalities in income and wealth. Zero-hours contracts can lead to health inequalities because they are a cause of in-work poverty.

Do you know?

1 List the major reasons why health inequality exists.
2 What effect do our lifestyle choices have on our health?
3 What is the connection between our genetics and our health?
4 How can the houses we live in cause health inequalities?

2.3 Effect of inequality on groups in society

You need to know
- how to evaluate the impact of social inequality on a group in society that you have studied
- how to evaluate the view that social inequality affects some groups in society more than others

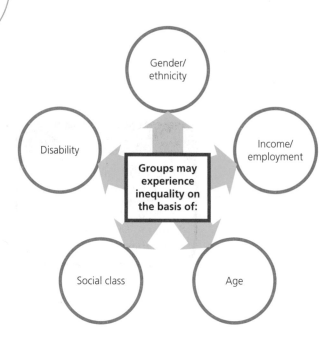

Exam tip

■ When answering exam questions on inequality, you should identify groups in society that experience inequality and describe the nature of this inequality. You should also provide balanced analytical/ evaluative comments on the effect of inequality on groups in society.

■ The diagram shows some possible approaches but these are not compulsory and the list is not exhaustive.

Gender inequality

■ Women experience inequality in relation to several factors:
- ☐ income
- ☐ age
- ☐ employment
- ☐ gender stereotyping
- ☐ education
- ☐ housing
- ☐ health
- ☐ social mobility

Exam tip

This list shows some possible approaches but these are not compulsory and the list is not exhaustive.

Income

■ More women than men are in jobs that pay the national minimum wage.
■ In many sectors, women earn less than men in equivalent employment.
■ Consequently, women are more likely to have smaller pensions.
■ However, gender pay-gap issues are being reduced and have halved in the last decade.

Synoptic link

Gender-based health inequality is related to gender-based income and wealth inequality. Look back at Section 2.2 on health inequality – low-paid or part-time work can lead to in-work poverty, which is a major cause of health inequality.

Age

■ The gender pay gap is smaller for workers aged between 20 and 30.
■ It increases considerably for those over 30.

Employment

- Women are more likely than men to be in low-paid or part-time work.
- Women account for over three-quarters of all jobs in the health and social work sector.
- They are more likely to work in the low-paid 'five Cs' – caring, catering, cleaning, clerical and cashiering.
- Around 20 per cent of small- and medium-sized enterprises (SMEs) are led by women (80 per cent are led by men).
- 29 per cent of directors of **FTSE 100** companies are women (71 per cent of directors are men).

Key term

FTSE 100 Stands for 'Financial Times Stock Exchange'; relates to Britain's 100 largest public companies.

Gender stereotyping

- Men and women can be unfairly stereotyped. Examples of attributes assigned to them are shown in the table below.

Attributes assigned to women	Attributes assigned to men
Emotional	Rational
Caring	Career-driven
In need of protection	

- As a result, gender stereotyping can affect a person's:
  - ☐ self-perception
  - ☐ well-being
  - ☐ participation in the world of work

Education

- At school, gender stereotyping can affect a person's:
  - ☐ treatment in the classroom
  - ☐ level and/or sense of achievement
  - ☐ academic performance
  - ☐ choice of subjects

Exam tip

In a 12-mark question, you should only refer to one distinct group because you will only be credited for the one which attracts the highest mark, and so referring to another will only waste time.

Ethnic inequality

- BME groups experience inequality in relation to several factors:
  - ☐ employment
  - ☐ income
  - ☐ wealth
  - ☐ education/qualifications
  - ☐ housing
  - ☐ health
  - ☐ social mobility

Exam tip

This list shows some possible approaches but these are not compulsory and the list is not exhaustive.

Employment

- Figure 2.1 shows the effect of inequality in employment between different ethnic groups.

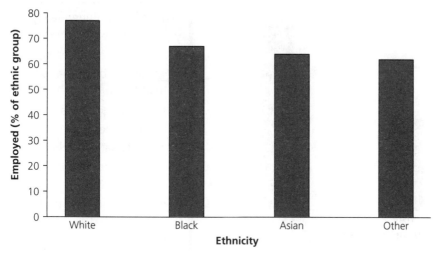

Figure 2.1 Percentage employment in the UK by ethnicity (2018)

- Note that there is at least a 10 per cent difference between the employment rate for white people and people from BME groups.

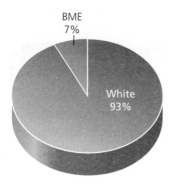

Figure 2.2 Schoolteachers in Scotland by ethnicity (2018)

- Figure 2.2 shows the disproportionately low number of BME that were employed in Scotland in 2018. This is because:
  - ☐ students from BME backgrounds are not being attracted into Initial Teacher Education
  - ☐ BME teachers experience a lack of opportunities to gain promoted posts
- The EIS reported that racism and discrimination can be found in schools, including Islamophobia, the use of racist or Islamophobic language, racist attitudes from colleagues, invisibility of racial diversity within curriculum content, curriculum content that perpetuated racial stereotypes and racist attitudes and comments from parents and pupils.

Wealth

- Figure 2.3 shows that twice as many BME groups are in poverty compared to white people in Scotland.

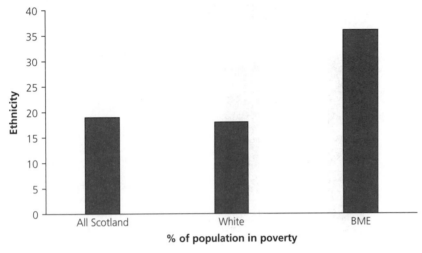

Figure 2.3 Poverty in Scotland by ethnicity (2018)

Effect of inequality on groups in society

- Inequality between groups in society can result in:

  - ☐ health issues
  - ☐ poverty
  - ☐ social exclusion
  - ☐ unemployment
  - ☐ **NEETs**
  - ☐ part-time work
  - ☐ low pay/income

  - ☐ homelessness
  - ☐ lack of education
  - ☐ high crime levels
  - ☐ gender stereotyping
  - ☐ discrimination
  - ☐ unstable family structure

- Women, disabled people and BME groups are less likely to be in work, often earn less than other workers and are less likely to get promoted.
- Female modern apprentices get paid less than males, and are usually persuaded to take up stereotypical apprenticeships like hairdressing while males take up construction-based ones, reinforcing income and wealth inequalities.
- Apprenticeships are difficult to come by for BME and disability groups. In Scotland in 2018:
  - ☐ BME people made up 4 per cent of the population, yet only 2 per cent started a modern apprenticeship
  - ☐ 20 per cent of working-age Scots had a disability, yet only half that (10 per cent) started a modern apprenticeship

Exam tip

It is worth remembering for the exam that, since all groups experience the same effects of inequality, you could approach these questions by considering:
- gender inequality and health issues
- ethnic inequality and health issues
- age inequality: child poverty and health issues
- inequality in relation to crime, education and housing.

Key term

NEET Stands for 'not in education, employment or training', specifically young people in this situation.

Synoptic link

There is clear link between health inequality and income/wealth inequality. Those on lower incomes find it harder to afford good quality, nutritious food and often work longer hours, sometimes skipping meals and not having enough time or energy left to exercise, leading to poor overall health.

Do you know?

1 Name three groups who may experience inequality.
2 Give three factors related to inequality for women.
3 Give three factors related to inequality for BME groups.
4 Which ethnic group has the highest employment rate in the UK?
5 Which ethnic group is most likely be in poverty in Scotland?

2.4 Individualist and collectivist debate

You need to know

■ how to evaluate the view that government should be responsible for tackling social inequality

- ■ There are two main theories for tackling social inequality: **individualist** and **collectivist**.
- ■ Individualist theories argue that:
  - □ Individuals should be responsible for providing their own housing, healthcare, education and pensions.
  - □ Individuals should be responsible for tackling their own social inequality, whereas the government should only play a small role.
- ■ Collectivist theories argue that:
  - □ The government should be responsible for tackling social inequality by providing for people who are unemployed, in poverty and facing inequality.
  - □ Inequality and poverty are caused by factors outside the control of the individual (such as unemployment and low pay). The government is responsible for helping to reduce the impact of these factors.
- ■ However, some argue that the collectivist theory only creates a 'dependency culture', where people become reliant on the government for their income and do not seek out opportunities to provide for themselves.
- ■ This is sometimes known as the 'nanny state'.

Key terms

Individualist The individual should be responsible for their own welfare.

Collectivist The government should be responsible for providing welfare.

Do you know?

1 Explain the theories put forward by individualists on how to tackle social inequality.
2 Explain the theories put forward by collectivists on how to tackle social inequality.

2.5 Tackling inequality

You need to know

■ the effectiveness of measures taken to tackle inequality, including government measures

Exam tip

When answering questions on tackling inequality, you must describe recent government policies that have targeted social and economic inequalities.

Measures to tackle inequalities

UK Government

Strategy	Effective because ...	Ineffective because ...
Reducing debt and expanding the economy	A strong economy means more money raised from tax that the government can use to increase investment to tackle inequality, e.g. in health and education	Despite output in the UK economy returning to pre-recession levels by 2014, some commentators argue that many people are worse off than they were in 2008. The unemployment rate at the start of 2016 was lower than the levels seen before the economic crash but many middle-income earners have seen their income squeezed. Wage rises have not kept up with inflation, making this group relatively poorer
Raising the tax threshold	Raising the level before which people pay tax on their earnings means take-home pay increases and many low earners don't need to pay any tax, so income inequality is reduced	Raising the level does not always help those on low incomes because pensioners and some part-time workers who didn't pay income tax before the threshold rise see no difference in their take-home pay
Living wage	The living wage is higher than the national minimum wage, helping to lower in-work poverty and reduce income inequality	It will cost jobs. Having to pay a wage above the market rate can lead employers to create fewer jobs and offer fewer hours to workers. This mostly affects unskilled manual workers. Ironically, those who benefit from the living wage are not the poor
The 'Big Society'	The government, voluntary sector and local communities work together to tackle inequality to make society better and fairer	It is seen as being a way to reduce welfare by replacing state support with voluntary support. This can be seen by the huge increase in the number of food banks in the UK
'Help to Work' scheme	Provides full-time unpaid placements for the long-term unemployed who work for their benefits	Those on the scheme are at risk of losing their benefits if they break the rules – 4 weeks' worth of jobseeker's allowance the first time and 3 months of benefits the second time

Exam tips

■ When answering questions on tackling inequality, you must describe recent government policies that have targeted social and economic inequalities.

■ You must also provide balanced analytical/evaluative comments on the effectiveness of government policies in reducing social and economic inequality and provide a clear, coherent line of argument.

Welfare

■ For some of those dependent on state benefits, there have been reductions in entitlement or payments under universal credit.

■ In 2019, the Work and Pensions Secretary linked universal credit to a rise in food bank use.

Universal credit

■ This is a benefit payment to help with living costs for those on a low income or out of work. It replaces the following benefits:
  □ child tax credit
  □ housing benefit
  □ income support
  □ income-based jobseeker's allowance (JSA)
  □ income-related employment and support allowance (ESA)
  □ working tax credit

Exam tip

■ If you write about the role of the UK benefit system in tackling inequality, you must also analyse/evaluate its successes/shortcomings in tackling social inequality.

■ If you write about the role of health services (public and/or private) in tackling inequality, you must also analyse/ evaluate their successes/ shortcomings in tackling social inequality.

Scottish Government

Addressing income and wealth inequality

'Achieving Our Potential' framework	
'Make work pay' by …	■ providing skills and training for people to progress in or into work ■ supporting economic development ■ creating employment opportunities
Maximise the potential for people to work by …	■ removing barriers to employment ■ providing affordable childcare
Maximise income for all by …	■ ensuring that everyone has a decent standard of living whether or not they are in work
Other measures	
Educational maintenance allowance (EMA)	provides financial support to assist young people from poorer backgrounds stay on at school to reduce educational inequality
Abolition of tuition fees	has reduced inequality in higher education by reducing the costs to university students, thus removing barriers to poorer students
Modern apprenticeship scheme	provides many young people with the skills to access employment and allows them to earn a living as they train
Free prescriptions and reduction of some hospital car-parking fees	have reduced what is seen as a tax on ill-health

- Unfortunately, the strategies for tackling income and wealth inequality have not been very effective overall.
- Despite significant investment in tackling health inequalities in Scotland, the gap between rich and poor remains.
- In 2018, almost half a million Scots were paid less than the living wage, with underpaid women outnumbering men by around 100,000.
- Around 1 in 4 Scottish children live in poverty.
- In 2018, 2 per cent more Scots were living in relative poverty than in 2017.
- In 2019, those living in deprived areas are still more likely to die early than those in wealthy areas.
- Scotland has the worst life expectancy in the UK and in 2019 it fell for first time in 35 years.
- Girls born in Scotland in 2017 can expect to live to 81.1 years and boys 77 years.
- In England, life expectancy for girls is 2 years higher and for boys it is 2.5 years higher.
- Critics have said that public health campaigns to tackle smoking, alcohol, diet and lack of exercise could increase health inequalities rather than reduce them due to lack of uptake by the poorest in society.
- The least well-off often have the poorest access to primary health services, cannot afford gym memberships and find it difficult to eat healthily because of the availability of cheap unhealthy foods.
- Welfare reform has left the poorest with smaller incomes, thereby increasing health and well-being inequalities.
- According to Child Poverty Action Group Scotland, this is because working families claiming universal credit receive significantly less financial support than before.
- Compared to the previous benefit system in Scotland, after universal credit was introduced:
  - □ couples with children became £960 a year worse off
  - □ lone-parent families became £2380 a year worse off
  - □ families with one child became £930 a year worse off
  - □ families with two children became £1100 a year worse off
  - □ families with three children became £2540 a year worse off

Addressing health inequality

- Health is a devolved matter, so in Scotland decisions on health are made by the Scottish Parliament.

Scottish Government strategy	Description of aim
'Equally well'	Helping to reduce health inequalities
NHS healthcare quality strategy	Reducing inequality by ensuring everyone can access healthcare services, regardless of their background or location
Minimum pricing for alcohol and the Alcohol Scotland Act	Reducing alcohol-related health issues by banning multibuy alcohol sales and some types of alcohol promotions and advertising
Smoking ban	Reducing smoking-related health issues by banning smoking in public places and cigarette displays, and enforcing plain packaging on cigarettes
'Healthy eating, active living'	Promoting healthy diets and increased physical activity and tackling obesity
'A route map towards healthy weight'	Reducing obesity levels
Partnership for Action on Drugs in Scotland (PADS)	Reducing drug use in Scotland
'Know the score' and 'The road to recovery'	Tackling drugs misuse

Addressing gender and racial inequality

Scottish Government strategy	Description of aim
The Equality Act	Legal protection of the rights of all groups, reducing gender and race discrimination
The equality duty	Promote equality of opportunity for all disadvantaged groups
Flexible working hours	Ensure all workers have the right to request flexible working hours
The 'One Scotland' campaign	Reduce racism
Ethnic Minority Employment Task Force	Reduce unemployment for BME groups
'Job fit'	Help those from BME groups to find work

Do you know?

1 Give three ways the UK Government tries to reduce income and wealth inequality.

2 Give three ways the Scottish Government tries to reduce income and wealth inequality.

3 Give two strategies of the Scottish Government to tackle health inequality.

4 Give two attempts by the Scottish Government to reduce gender and race inequality.

End of section 2 questions

Option 1

1 Explain the reasons for gender and ethnic inequality.

2 Outline how it is possible to be in work yet be in poverty.

3 Explain the reasons why poverty can lead to health inequality.

4 Outline the main effects of inequality on women, BME groups and disabled people.

5 Outline the effectiveness of measures taken by the UK Government to tackle inequality.

6 Outline the effectiveness of measures taken by the Scottish Government to address income and wealth inequality.

7 Describe the measures used by the Scottish Government to address health inequality.

Option 2 Crime and the law
2.6 Legal rights and responsibilities of citizens

You need to know

■ the legal rights and responsibilities of UK citizens
■ categories of crimes and offences

Legal rights of UK citizens

■ **Presumption of innocence**:
  □ Anyone accused of a crime is presumed to be innocent until it has been proven they are guilty.
  □ This means that they do not have to prove that they are innocent; instead it must be proven that they are guilty.
■ **The right to legal aid**: this pays for a lawyer to represent the accused in court.
■ **The right to a fair trial**: a fair, public trial that is heard by an impartial and independent court or tribunal 'within a reasonable time'.

Responsibilities of UK citizens

- respect the rights of other citizens
- pay taxes
- vote in elections
- obey the law
- undertake jury service

Exam tip

In the exam you can refer to relevant and contemporary aspects of crime, criminology and the law in either Scotland **or** the UK, **or** both Scotland **and** the UK.

Categories of crimes and offences

- Crimes can be covered by **civil law** or **criminal law**.
  - □ Civil law is about the rights and responsibilities of individuals and organisations. It deals with disputes between people, and other organisations, for example, family matters, neighbour disputes and employment issues.
  - □ Criminal law covers more series crimes such as murder, rape and robbery and some minor crimes like speeding and causing a disturbance in the street.
- Crime in Scotland is categorised using five groups (see the table below and Figure 2.4).

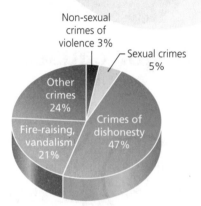

Figure 2.4 **Types of crime committed in Scotland (%)**

Category of crime	Type of crime
Non-sexual crimes of violence	- Murder - Robbery
Sexual crimes	- Rape
Crimes of dishonesty	- Housebreaking - Theft - Shoplifting
Fire-raising, vandalism	- Malicious mischief - Reckless conduct
Other crimes	- Possession of an offensive weapon - Possession and supply of controlled drugs

Do you know?

1 Give three legal rights of UK citizens.
2 What is meant by the term 'presumption of innocence'?
3 Give three responsibilities of UK citizens.

2.7 Causes and theories of crime

You need to know

- the causes of crimes
- the theories behind why crimes happen (biological, psychological and sociological; individualist free choice versus collectivist socialisation theories)

Major causes of crime

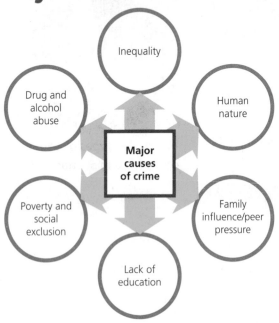

Theories of crime

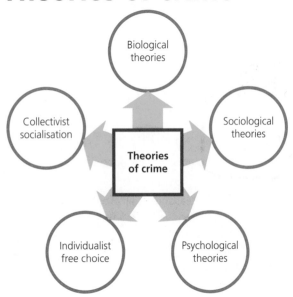

Exam tip

When answering question on the causes and theories of crime, you should also provide analytical/ evaluative comments referring to each cause or theory and their relative importance.

Biological theories

■ Biological theories say that some people are 'born criminals' and are physically different to non-criminals.

Biological theory of crime	Explanation of main points
Lombroso theory	There are physical differences between criminals and non-criminals, and criminal tendencies are inherited
Sheldon's theory of body types	There are three different human body types: ■ ectomorphs (thin and fragile) ■ endomorphs (soft and fat) ■ mesomorphs (muscular and athletic) According to Sheldon's theory, those with a mesomorph body type are the most likely to be criminals
Y-chromosome theory	Criminals have an extra Y-chromosome that causes them to commit crimes

Exam tip

You can gain marks by referring to links between factors such as drug and/or alcohol abuse, peer influence or family influence, even if you don't specifically mention theorists.

Sociological theories

■ Sociological theories say that society creates criminals.
■ They state that criminals are drawn to crime by external social factors that influence them, such as their family and friends and where they live.

Sociological theory of crime	Explanation of main points
Strain theory (Emile Durkheim/Robert Merton)	Crime is caused because of the strain on people who lack the money, employment or education to achieve wealth and status. This strain creates criminals who are pushed into crime to get what they want
Labelling theory (Howard Becker)	Certain groups that are labelled as being 'deviant' are more likely to commit crimes as a result. Attaching negative labels to groups (e.g. age or race) can stigmatise them and influence them to adopt their labelled behaviour and commit crimes
Social control theory (Travis Hirschi)	People are less likely to commit crime if they have strong social bonds, but are more likely if they have weak social bonds

Psychological theories

■ Psychological theories say that individuals are responsible for their own behaviour and that criminals act based on their own individual personality.

Psychological theory of crime	Explanation of main points
Psychoanalytic theory (Sigmund Freud)	Everyone has criminal tendencies which are normally supressed. When they are not, it can lead to criminal behaviour
Cognitive development theory	Criminals have not developed sufficient reasoning skills to help them make moral decisions. Their criminal behaviour is seen as a defect in moral thinking, thought processes and mental development

Individualist free choice versus collectivist socialisation theories

- Advocates of individualist free choice theories would argue that:
  - ☐ individuals in pursuit of their own self-interest are responsible for their own behaviour and actions
  - ☐ thus they should be prepared to suffer the consequences for those actions
- Advocates of collectivist socialisation theories would argue that:
  - ☐ external factors influence the behaviour and actions of individuals
  - ☐ thus society has a responsibility to create fair and equal communities that will ultimately deter crime

Individualist principles	Collectivist principles
Place a strong emphasis on individual rights	Place a strong emphasis on the role of the state
It is the responsibility of the individual to respect and not break the law	Everyone has a shared responsibility towards wider society
The individual has the freedom to pursue their own self-interests within the bounds of the law	Everyone has a shared responsibility to actively contribute as good citizens and hold the government accountable for society
Individuals should be responsible for themselves	As citizens, we have a shared responsibility for each other and to create a better society

Do you know?

1 Give three major causes of crime.
2 Give three major theories of crime.
3 What do biological theories of crime say?
4 What do sociological theories of crime say?
5 What do psychological theories of crime say?

2.8 Impact on victims, offenders and their families

You need to know

- the impact of crime on victims, offenders, the families of victims and the families of offenders

Impact on the victim

Effect	Examples
Financial loss/loss of income	<ul><li>Victims may lose money or belongings if they are mugged or their home is burgled</li><li>They may have to take time off work, resulting in a loss of earnings, or may be unable to return to work, causing them to become unemployed or unemployable</li></ul>
Loss of confidence/ physical suffering	<ul><li>Victims may experience a lack of self-esteem, especially as a result of sexual crimes</li><li>They may have sustained physical injuries and scarring that might alter their appearance, reducing their self-confidence</li><li>They may develop anxiety disorders like post-traumatic stress disorder (PTSD), leaving them feeling scared emotionally and/or causing panic attacks</li><li>Victims may self-harm if they are feeling anxious, depressed or stressed</li><li>Some find it difficult to sleep and don't eat properly, which affects their general health</li></ul>
Psychological effects	<ul><li>Short-term effects include victims feeling afraid, angry and depressed</li><li>Long-term effects include victims not being able to sleep, having anxiety attacks or reliving the event (that can lead to PTSD)</li></ul>
Social effects	<ul><li>Victims can be forced to go through a lifestyle change as a result of crime, e.g. moving house, changing habits and avoiding places or types of travel</li></ul>

Impact on the offender

Impact	Examples
Financial penalty/ unemployment	<ul><li>Offenders may have to pay a fine or make compensation</li><li>They may lose their job and become unable to get a new job because they have a criminal record</li></ul>
Imprisonment	<ul><li>Offenders may lose their home and job because they are in prison</li></ul>
Loss of status and/ or respect	<ul><li>Offenders may feel shame and guilt for their actions</li><li>They may experience relationship stresses, leading to break-ups and/or divorce</li><li>They may become socially excluded and ignored by friends and society</li></ul>

Exam tip

When answering questions on the impact of crime, you should describe and explain the impact of crime on victims and their families, and offenders and their families.

Impact on families of victims

- Victims' families may go through a mix of emotional states, such as feelings of anxiety, anger, confusion and may react in unusual ways.
- They may be unable to control their own emotions, becoming tearful, or feel overwhelmed, afraid or helpless and unable to cope.
- Some may also feel afraid about what to do or afraid to leave the house.
- Some families of victims also suffer sleeplessness and nightmares, which can further impact their mental health and ability to cope.
- Families of victims may experience financial hardship or poverty and can fall into debt, especially if the victim was the main household earner and can no longer work

Exam tip

Make sure you provide balanced analytical/ evaluative comments referring to the relative impact of crime on the individuals and (depending on the specific question) the wider community, society, the economy, government etc.

Impact on families of offenders

- Offenders' families can experience emotional and financial disruption to their life.
- Family relationships can be put under strain, leading to separation, divorce and even suicide.
- If a loved one is imprisoned these issues may have a greater impact, as families may be emotionally distressed by their absence.
- Families may experience financial hardship or poverty and can fall into debt, especially if the offender was the main earner of the household, due to imprisonment or the offender losing their job.
- They may also find themselves stigmatised by neighbours, the community or wider society because they are deemed 'guilty by association', causing them to lose status and/or respect and even leading to social exclusion.

Synoptic link

The impact of crime has links to and is similar to the impact of terrorism, which can be useful for the exam if you have chosen terrorism as your world issue.

Do you know?

1 Give three personal impacts of crime on victims.
2 Give three personal impacts of crime on offenders.
3 Give three impacts of crime on the families of victims.
4 Give three impacts of crime on the families of offenders.

2.9 Social and economic impact on society

You need to know

- the economic impact of crime on wider society
- the social impact of crime on wider society
- how to evaluate the economic impact of crime on society

Economic impact

- For just 1 year in Scotland, the economic and social cost of crime is almost £3000 million.
- This places a burden on both tax-paying citizens and the government to afford the financial cost of crime.
- Moreover, this is money that could potentially have been spent elsewhere, such as investment in welfare or business.

Table 2.1 Economic cost of crime in Scotland (2016)

Category of crime	Cost (£ million)
Non-sexual crimes of violence	414.8
Sexual crimes	1,629.9
Crimes of dishonesty	447.1
Fire-raising and vandalism	350.4
Other crimes	140.9
Total	2,983.1

Social impact

- Crime can make a community feel distressed and unsafe, whether it's from antisocial behaviour like littering, vandalism, noisy neighbours or alcohol-related antisocial behaviour.
- 82 per cent of the wider community in Scotland feel that the social impact of alcohol abuse is 'a big problem', while 16 per cent feel that it is 'a bit of a problem' and only 2 per cent feel that it's 'not a problem'.
- Many people feel threatened by drunkards and are offended by them urinating and vomiting in the street.

- In 2018, consuming alcohol in a public place was the second most commonly issued antisocial behaviour Fixed Penalty Notice (FPN).
- High crime levels in an area can have negative impacts on people and communities, such as:
  - ☐ fear – people don't feel safe to walk the streets or leave the house
  - ☐ high levels of violence
  - ☐ antisocial behaviour
  - ☐ vandalism/graffiti
  - ☐ drop in house prices in the area, or difficulties selling a house
  - ☐ increase in home insurance costs
  - ☐ lack of investment from businesses, which in turn leads to:
    - loss of jobs
    - unemployment
    - poverty

Do you know?

1 What is the economic and social cost of crime over 1 year in Scotland?
2 Which crime had the highest economic cost in Scotland in 2016?
3 Give three negative impacts on communities that high levels of crime can cause.

2.10 Custodial and non-custodial responses

You need to know
- the differences between custodial and non-custodial responses to crime
- the effectiveness of non-custodial sentences in Scotland

Custodial responses

- Custodial sentences include prison sentences or being sent to a young offender institution.

- A short-term custodial (prison) sentence is less than 4 years. Those given a short-term prison sentence are usually released from prison after serving half their time but will complete the remainder of their sentence in the community.

- A long-term custodial (prison) sentence is 4 years or more. Those given a long-term prison sentence usually serve their whole time in prison except for the last 6 months.

Table 2.2 Scottish court sentencing options

| High Court | Sheriff Court | | Justice of the Peace Court |
	Solemn	Summary	
Prison sentence: any length	**Prison sentence:** up to 5 years	**Prison sentence:** up to 1 year	**Prison sentence:** up to 60 days
Community sentence: up to 3 years	**Community sentence:** up to 3 years	**Community sentence:** any length	Some **community sentences**
Fine: any amount	**Fine:** any amount	**Fine:** up to £10,000	**Fine:** up to £2,500
Community sentences include:			

- Restriction of liberty orders (RLOs)
- Community payback orders (CPOs)
- Bail supervision
- Presumption against prison
- Drug treatment and testing orders (DTTOs)
- Antisocial behaviour orders (ASBOs)

Non-custodial responses

- Non-custodial sentences are alternatives to prison sentences or young offender institutions, and include:
  - ☐ Fine
  - ☐ DTTO
  - ☐ CPO
  - ☐ RLO, e.g. electronic tagging
  - ☐ ASBO
  - ☐ Restorative justice

Effectiveness of non-custodial sentences

- In Scotland:
  - ☐ Almost one-third of offenders who receive a CPO commit another crime afterwards.
  - ☐ However, offenders who are given a short jail term have a reconviction rate that is double those given a CPO.
  - ☐ Also, those convicted of low-level crimes like shoplifting are more likely to be reconvicted than those who commit more serious crimes.
  - ☐ According to the Scottish Government, both the reconviction rate and the average number of reconvictions per offender have decreased since 2014.
  - ☐ Since 2014, the reconviction rate has fallen by around 1.5 per cent and the average number of reconvictions per offender has decreased by 6 per cent.
  - ☐ This has been put down to the efforts to rehabilitate offenders and help them turn from crime.

- These figures could be used to argue that short custodial sentences are not effective and do not work and that alternative community sentences are effective and do work.
- Community sentences offer a real alternative to custodial sentences by supporting offenders to deal with the personal issues behind offending behaviour.
- Around 90 per cent of women sent to prison get a sentence of less than a year. It is argued that they would be better off being cared for outside prison on CPOs or **bail supervision**.

Key term

Bail supervision Instead of being sent to prison, offenders are released on bail on the condition that they satisfy certain restrictions and conditions.

Do you know?

1 Give three examples of non-custodial sentences.
2 What is a short-term custodial sentence?
3 What is a long-term custodial sentence?

End of section 2 questions

Option 2

1 Explain three legal rights of UK citizens.
2 Explain the difference between civil law and criminal law.
3 Name the five categories of crime in Scotland and outline their associated types of crime.
4 Explain in detail the biological theory of crime.
5 Explain in detail the sociological theory of crime.
6 Explain in detail the psychological theory of crime.
7 Outline the main differences between the individualist free choice and collectivist socialisation theories of crime.
8 Explain the impact crime has on victims and their families.
9 Explain the impact crime has on offenders and their families.
10 Explain the social and economic impact of crime on wider society.
11 Discuss the effectiveness of non-custodial sentences in Scotland.

3 International issues

Option 1 World powers
3.1 Democratic participation

You need to know
- the extent to which the political system in your chosen world power allows democratic participation

- Factors that determine democratic participation in a world power include:
  - ☐ the extent of democracy in that world power
  - ☐ the nature and status of constitutional arrangements
  - ☐ the type of political system in place
  - ☐ the type and role of the electoral system used
  - ☐ the opportunity to vote in elections at different levels
  - ☐ ability to form, join and/or campaign for political parties
  - ☐ the opportunity to stand as a candidate in elections
  - ☐ the opportunity for party activism
  - ☐ the opportunity to join a pressure or interest group
  - ☐ the opportunity to take part in pressure/interest group activities
  - ☐ the extent of human and political rights which operate
  - ☐ the opportunity to protest or take direct action
  - ☐ the role of the media

Exam tips

■ When answering questions on the topic of democratic participation, you should describe the **political** opportunities that exist for people to participate.

■ When answering questions on influencing government decision making, you should analyse how **political** opportunities can influence government decision making.

The USA

Table 3.1 Citizens' ability to influence US Government decision-making

Ability to influence government decision-making	Limits to influencing government decision-making
Citizens can vote in county, state and federal elections for positions such as local judge, dog catcher, sheriff, governor, senator and president	Convicted criminals are unable to register to vote, and there are barriers to some groups to registering to vote
Political rights of citizens are enshrined in the US Constitution	The political system over-represents affluent white males and under-represents women, ethnic minorities and the poor in the political process
Citizens can stand as a candidate in elections and join political parties and campaign for candidates and policies	There are differences in participation and registration rates between social classes and ethnic groups. The high cost of running and standing as a candidate automatically excludes poorer citizens
Citizens may choose to participate in interest groups, e.g.: ■ National Rifle Association (NRA) ■ Black Lives Matter ■ Occupy and Anonymous Movement Around 75 per cent of Americans belong to at least one interest group	Interest group influence is limited by lack of financial backing. Citizens have no legal right to join a trade union and membership is declining
Citizens may choose to participate in initiatives and referenda	Results are easily repealed or amended by legislature
Citizens have access to a variety of news and social movements (not just mainstream), including: ■ slacktivism ■ 4Chan (anonymous image-based bulletin board) ■ AltRight (an ultra-conservative, far-right movement in the US) ■ Breitbart News Network (a far-right syndicated American news, opinion and commentary website)	Criticisms exist that elected US politicians are acting as lobbyists for American business interests rather than fully representing the will of their electorate Abuse of social media including 'fake news' or misinformation intended to discredit or breed hostility

Key terms

Slacktivism Social media activism with very little personal effort.

National Rifle Association (NRA) US interest group advocating gun rights.

People's Republic of China

Table 3.2 Citizens' ability to influence Chinese Government decision making

Ability to influence government decision making	Limits to influencing government decision making
On paper, China has a liberal constitution that allows all citizens to vote and stand for election. It protects freedom of speech, freedom of assembly and the press	The People's Republic of China (PRC) endorses the Communist Party's control and supremacy over the political rights of citizens. There is no constitutional democracy
Elected officials at each level of government have decision-making powers, i.e. local, district, regional and national	Local elections are dominated by the CPC and all candidates must be approved by them
Citizens can vote at local level, but only candidates and parties sanctioned by the Communist Party of China (CPC) are allowed to run for election	Citizens can only vote at local level; they cannot vote for the president, state council or even for governors or mayors
Around 7 per cent of the Chinese population (85 million) are members of the CPC	There are restrictions on who is allowed to join the CPC (which is by invitation only)
There are eight legal democratic parties other than the CPC to choose from, such as the China Democratic League, and the Chinese Peasants' and Workers' Democratic Party	▪ Other parties only exist with the permission of the CPC and cannot act as an opposition party ▪ The PRC operates as a one party-communist dictatorship ▪ The other eight 'democratic' parties are under the leadership of, and act as a rubber stamp of, the CPC
Citizens have access to the internet and social media sites through Baidu (an allowed search engine) and WeChat messenger (developed by Tencent, in China)	The internet is widely monitored and controlled by the state; many sites are prohibited and blocked by the 'great firewall of China' filtering system. Google is a blocked site in China
Citizens have access to a variety of television and radio stations	▪ There is censorship of all media. Access to foreign news is blocked/limited (e.g. BBC) ▪ China is ranked at 173 of 178 countries on the Press Freedom Index
Citizens have opportunities for protests and direct action, e.g. growth of pro-democracy movement in Hong Kong. Some pressure group activity and protests are tolerated provided they are not pro-democracy, e.g. environmental groups have grown in number, have experienced limited success and become popular	Suppression, censorship and imprisonment operate: ▪ Protests have to be sanctioned by the CPC and cannot question the authority or legitimacy of the Communist Party ▪ Any dissent is ruthlessly dealt with by security forces ▪ Many dissidents have been in prison since the 1989 Tiananmen Square protests and others have been exiled, e.g. Wei Jingshen (human rights activist)
There is a growing membership of the All-China Federation of Trade Unions, where members can campaign for workers' rights. The All-China Women's Federation gives women the opportunity to campaign for women's rights	Trade unions are not independent organisations and operate under the supervision of the CPC

Do you know?

1 Give five factors that determine the extent to which the political system in your chosen world power allows democratic participation.

2 Give five limits to the ways in which people in the USA **or** China can influence government decision making.

3 Give two ways in which people in the USA **or** China can influence government decision-making.

3.2 Political institutions and government decision making

You need to know

■ how the political institutions in your chosen world power work together to make decisions

USA

Features of the US Constitution

■ The US Constitution is based on the following ideas:

Republicanism	The USA is a republic, so power lies with the people who elect representatives to use this power on their behalf
Federalism	The USA is also a federal country, so power is split between national, state and local government
Separation of powers	Federal power is divided into three separate branches of government: ■ the executive (the president and his/her cabinet) ■ the legislature (two chambers of congress) ■ the judiciary (the supreme court)
'Checks and balances'	Through the separation of powers, each branch of government is reliant on the others to exercise full power. Consequently, each branch can limit the power of the others to prevent any one branch becoming too powerful

Exam tips

■ You will gain marks in the exam for giving detailed descriptions and explanations of how political institutions in your chosen world power can dominate government decision making or not.

■ You must also analyse/ evaluate how effective they are at influencing government decision-making.

3.2 Political institutions and government decision making

Branches of the US Government

- The US Government is divided into the executive, legislature and judiciary.

Executive

- The executive branch is responsible for enforcing the laws made by congress.
- The president leads the federal government.
- He/she is elected every 4 years and is not allowed to serve for more than two terms.
- He/she chooses his/her own cabinet members.

Legislature

- Congress passes legislation and the budget.
- It has two chambers: the Senate and the House of Representatives.
- There are 100 senators and 435 members of the House of Representatives.

Judiciary

- The US Supreme Court ensures that all legislation is constitutional.

Branch of US government	Main roles/responsibilities	Controlled by ...		
		Executive	Legislature	Judicial
Federal	Set taxes, spending and other national policies; take the decision to go to war	President	Congress	Supreme court
State	Manage hospitals and health care; build and repair roads; fund schools and colleges; collect taxes to pay for state police forces	Governor	State legislature	State courts
Local	Provide water and sewerage service; remove rubbish; clear snow; provide housing, schools and transport services; protect the public	Mayor	City council	Local courts

Separation of powers

- This is also known as a system of 'checks and balances', and prevents any branch from dominating government decision making.
- The president can only propose laws and a budget; congress must approve them.

Answers at **www.hoddereducation.co.uk/needtoknow/answers** 59

- If any of the president's proposals require money, he/she has to persuade congress to pay for it (e.g. President Donald Trump's Mexican wall) because only congress can impose taxes.
- Although the president is commander-in-chief of the armed forces and responsible for foreign policy, only congress can declare war and the senate must approve any treaties the president makes.
- The president can veto bills passed in congress, but this can be overridden if two-thirds of congress vote against it.
- The president can nominate judges and government officials for appointment but these have to be approved by the senate.

Two-party system

- The USA has a **two-party electoral system**, in which the main parties are the Democratic Party and the Republican Party.
- In the USA, this usually means that one of the parties controls the executive branch and one has a majority in the legislative branch of government.
- There are other parties in the US (e.g. the Reform Party, the Libertarian Party and the Green Party) but they have very little influence or impact.
- Every president since 1853 has been either a Democrat or a Republican.

Key term

Two-party electoral system A democratic system where only two parties continually win elections with a majority of votes.

Democrats	Republicans
Believe that government should have more control and be more involved in people lives	Believe that people should have more opportunities and control over their own lives
Believe that government has a responsibility to help those in need	Believe that politicians running the country should not get too involved
Value individual freedom and choice, e.g.: ■ pro gay marriage ■ pro immigration	Place importance on traditional values, including ■ law and order ■ pro armed forces ■ attending church
Receive more support in urban areas (large cities)	Receive more support in rural areas

People's Republic of China
Features of the Chinese constitution

■ The Chinese constitution is based on the following ideas:

Unitary system	Centralisation of powers in one government. Although there are provinces, autonomous regions and municipalities in China, these can be removed at any time
Democratic centralism	The National People's Congress (NPC) of the Communist Party of China is a government based on the principle of **democratic centralism**
Unicameral legislature	The NPC is the **unicameral legislature** (single legislative assembly) of China
Communist Party of China (CPC)	The CPC is at the centre of the executive, legislative and judicial branches. The government is under its control and nothing can be done either without its consent or against its will
A people's republic (People's Republic of China)	The people administer the affairs of state in accordance with the law

Branches of the Chinese Government

■ The Chinese Government is divided into the executive, legislature and judiciary.

Executive

Head of government	Premier and executive vice premiers
Cabinet	State council, appointed by the NPC
Elections/appointments	Premier and executive vice premier are indirectly elected by the NPC for a 5-year term (and may serve an unlimited number of terms)

Legislature

Unicameral	National People's Congress (NPC)
Cabinet	Members are indirectly elected by municipal, regional and provincial people's congresses, and by the People's Liberation Army
Elections/appointments	In practice, only members of the CPC and CPC-approved independent candidates are elected

Judiciary

Highest court	Supreme people's court
Elections/appointments	The chief justice is appointed by the NPC and may serve up to two consecutive 5-year terms

> **Key terms**
>
> **Democratic centralism**
> A system of organisation whereby policy is decided centrally and all members are bound to it.
>
> **Unicameral legislature** A system of government that has only one legislative chamber.

Political structure

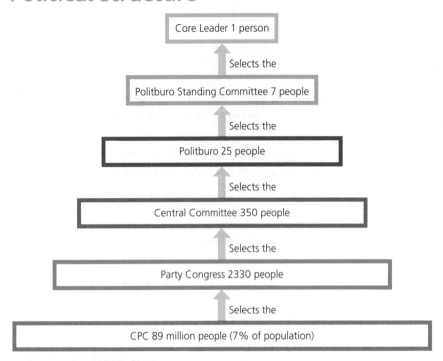

- The Chinese Communist Party (CPC) holds a monopoly on power, but only 7 per cent of China's total population are members.
- China's party system is based on **meritocracy**.
- However, the political system of China is also characterised by a one-party system – that is, the CPC.
- The core leader is head of the Politburo Standing Committee, which is the main decision-making body.
- The core leader is the president of the People's Republic of China but is also the general secretary of the CPC, the president of central government and the chief of the Central Military Commission.
- However, the core leader does face constraints on their power.

> ### Key term
>
> **Meritocracy** A system whereby the governing people in society are chosen according to merit.

'Checks and balances'

- The CPC has two opposing factions:
  - ☐ the Communist Youth League of China
  - ☐ the Princelings
- The Communist Youth League is more populist, whereas the Princelings are more elitist.
- The two factions check each other in the power struggle and balance each other with their different skillsets and backgrounds.

Political cycle

- China holds a party congress every 5 years.
- Leadership roles have a two-term limit.
- The core leader normally consolidates their power in the first term and implements their political agenda in the second term.

Do you know?

1 List the four main features of the US Constitution **or** the Chinese constitution.

2 What are the three main branches of the US Government **or** the Chinese Government?

3 Answer **a** or **b**.

  a What are the two main political parties in the USA?

  b What is the main political party in China?

3.3 Socio-economic inequality

You need to know

- how socio-economic inequality manifests itself in your chosen world power
- how people are affected by socio-economic inequality

Exam tip

For questions in this section of the exam, you should identify and describe areas where there is socio-economic inequality in the world power you have studied.

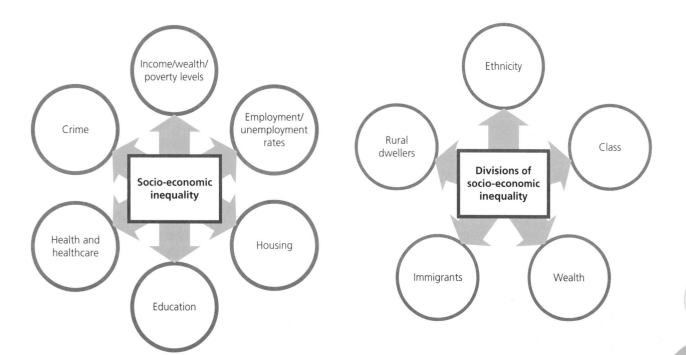

USA

Socio-economic inequality

Income

- The gap between the rich and poor is increasing.
- 40 per cent of Americans live in poverty.
- Black and Hispanic people are more likely to have lower household incomes than white and Asian American people, and thus experience higher poverty levels.
- Black people are almost three times more likely to be living in poverty than white people.
- However, there is a growing middle class among African Americans, who:
  - ☐ report higher salaries
  - ☐ have been able to 'lift' themselves out of poverty
  - ☐ have been able to move to better neighbourhoods, which have better access to education and employment opportunities (such as Atlanta and Los Angeles)

Education

- Black and Hispanic people have higher dropout rates than white and Asian American people.
- A 'funding gap' is evident in schools in deprived areas which are mostly attended by ethnic minority groups, leading to inequalities in educational attainment.

Health

- Black and Hispanic people are more likely to have no health insurance compared to white people.
- Illnesses related to overall health are evident within these ethnic groups. For example, 50 per cent of African Americans are classed as obese and report lower life expectancies.

Crime

- There is a disproportionate make-up of prison population by ethnicity, with black and Hispanic people in the majority.

Immigrants

- Both legal and illegal immigrants experience many social and economic inequalities, such as:
  - ☐ low wage rates
  - ☐ long working hours
  - ☐ poor housing conditions

> **Exam tip**
>
> You must also analyse/evaluate the ways in which groups of society have been affected. Issues you should refer to can include income/wealth and health inequalities including poverty levels, employment/unemployment rates, housing, education, healthcare and crime.

People's Republic of China
Socio-economic inequality

Income

- Income inequality is growing.
- China has 613 cities which are usually divided into six tiers that describe their relative level of development. Tier 1 cities are most developed, and tier 6 cities are least developed.
- The number of wage earners in tier 1 and 2 cities is higher than in other cities in China, adding to income inequality.

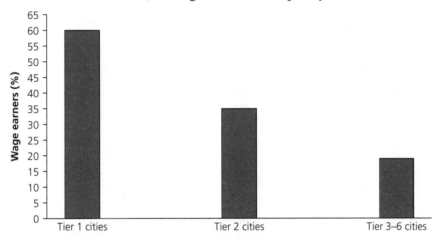

Figure 3.1 Wage earners in China's cities (by tier)

- Rural residents have an annual average disposable income that is less than one-third of the average disposable income of urban residents.
- This difference has been growing since 1978 and is set to continue.
- The richest 1 per cent of Chinese households own 33 per cent of China's wealth.
- The poorest 25 per cent of Chinese households own 1 per cent of China's wealth.
- China's **Gini coefficient** for income was 0.47 in 2017, where anything above 0.40 indicates severe income inequality (for comparison, Germany's was 0.3).
- In China, the Gini coefficient has risen more steeply over the last 10 years than in any other country.

Key term

Gini coefficient A widely used measure of inequality.

Employment/unemployment

■ 9.68 million people in China are unemployed.

■ 77.586 million people in China are in employment.

Ethnicity

■ Not all ethnic minority groups are treated in the same way.

■ The more 'loyal' a group is to the Chinese state and the more integrated it is into the culture and economy, the better its members will be treated.

■ Tibetan and Uighur people, who continue to challenge the Chinese Government's plans for their homelands, are treated poorly.

■ Many Tibetans accuse the Chinese Government of suppressing Tibetan culture, freedom of expression and worship.

■ The Chinese Government and individual Han Chinese citizens have been accused of discrimination against the Uighur minority, who are 're-educated' – forced to speak Mandarin and to support the CPC.

Education

■ China's urban–rural differences cause inequalities in access to education.

■ In 2018, 97 per cent of girls in rural areas had enrolled in primary education, but only 79 per cent went on to attend secondary school.

■ This has been blamed in part on lower parental expectations and fewer employment opportunities for women in rural areas.

■ At China's top universities, gender inequality also exists.

■ In 2018, the female-to-male ratio at Peking University was 47 to 53.

■ However, women are more likely to study abroad than men.

■ In 2018, 63 per cent of Chinese students in the UK were female and 51 per cent of Chinese students in the USA were female.

Health

■ Life expectancy of people in China:
  □ males: 73.7 years
  □ females: 78.1 years
  □ average for total population: 75.8 years

Table 3.3 Availability of healthcare in China (per 1000 people)

Resource	Urban areas	Rural areas
Doctors	4	1.5
Nurses	5	1.5
Hospital beds	8.5	4

Crime

Table 3.4 Percentage make-up of sexual murder crimes and those incarcerated

Sexual murderers	Sexual murder victims	Prison population
97% males	83% female	6.5% female
67% single males		0.8% young offenders
68% educated to secondary school level		0.4% foreign nationals

Migrants

- China has around 250 million rural migrant workers, of which about 150 million are believed to work outside their registered home area.
- Migrant workers experience:
  - low wage rates
  - long working hours
  - poor housing conditions
  - loss of welfare benefits associated with the household registration system (known as hukou)

Access to drinking water

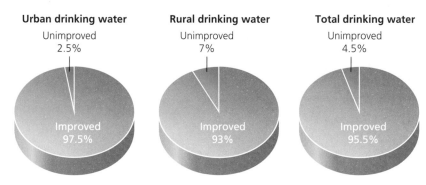

Figure 3.2 Quality of drinking water

- Improved drinking water includes use of any of the following sources:
  - piped water into a dwelling, yard or plot
  - public tap or standpipe
  - tubewell or borehole
  - protected dug well
  - protected spring
  - rainwater collection
- Unimproved drinking water includes use of any of the following sources:
  - unprotected dug well
  - unprotected spring

- ☐ cart with small tank or drum
- ☐ tanker truck
- ☐ surface water, including rivers, dams, lakes, ponds, streams, canals or irrigation channels
- ☐ bottled water

Access to good sanitation

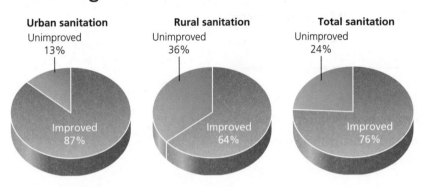

Figure 3.3 Quality of sanitation

- ■ Improved sanitation includes use of any of the following facilities:
  - ☐ flush or pour-flush to a piped sewer system, septic tank or pit latrine
  - ☐ ventilated improved pit (VIP) latrine
  - ☐ pit latrine with slab
  - ☐ a composting toilet
- ■ Unimproved sanitation includes use of any of the following facilities:
  - ☐ flush or pour-flush not piped to a sewer system, septic tank or pit latrine
  - ☐ pit latrine without a slab or an open pit
  - ☐ bucket
  - ☐ hanging toilet or hanging latrine
  - ☐ shared facilities of any type
  - ☐ no facilities
  - ☐ a bush or field

Do you know?

1 Which group in the USA **or** China is most likely to experience income inequality?

2 Which groups in the USA **or** China are more likely to experience health inequality?

3 Which groups in the USA **or** China are more likely to experience educational inequality?

4 Which groups in the USA **or** China are more likely to experience crime inequality?

5 In what ways do immigrants in the USA **or** migrants in China experience inequality?

3.4 Government responses to socio-economic inequality

You need to know

- government responses to economic inequality
- government responses to educational inequality
- government responses to employment inequality

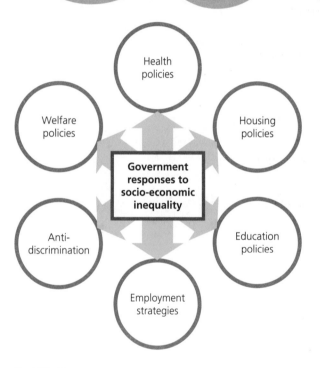

Exam tips

- When answering questions on this topic, you should describe government action that is aimed at tackling inequality.

- You should also analyse or evaluate the successes and/or shortcomings of this action.

USA

Government responses to inequality

Economic

Welfare to Work

- Welfare to Work is the main US Government strategy to reduce poverty.
- Welfare support, such as Medicaid health insurance, childcare, food stamps and earned income tax credit (EITC), is linked to finding work.
- This scheme has encouraged more people into work, which has increased the incomes of the poorest and reduced the cost of the welfare budget.
- However, it has forced many people to work for very low wages and has not reduced inequality or poverty levels in the USA.

Temporary Assistance to Needy Families (TANF)

- TANF aims to help single parents into work.
- Since TANF was introduced, the child poverty rate among single parents has fallen.
- However, there are fewer families receiving TANF as eligibility rules have been tightened.
- Overall child poverty levels are still high and are one of the highest in the developed world.

Education

Every Student Succeeds Act

- This has reduced educational inequality by supporting disadvantaged groups.
- It has raised academic standards and helped prepare students to succeed in college and work.
- High school graduation rates are now at all-time highs and dropout rates are at historic lows, with more students going to college than ever before.
- However, the new Act was meant to give power back to individual states and it is claimed that this has not happened.
- It has also been claimed that there has been little change or improvement as a result.

Employment

- Government strategies to tackle employment inequality include:
  - ☐ Affirmative Action (AA) in employment
  - ☐ laws to ensure companies with more than 50 employees do not practice discrimination in not hiring or promoting people from disadvantaged groups
  - ☐ contracts being given to companies that are minority-owned or employ large numbers of people from disadvantaged groups
- These strategies have helped minority groups to overcome social and economic disadvantage and discrimination and have helped to create a fairer society, for example, the rise of the black middle classes.
- However, they assign help by race, not ability, and are seen as 'reverse discrimination' by some white people.
- Businesses feel forced to employ and promote people from minority groups who are not always the best candidate for the job.

People's Republic of China

- China has moved from being a moderately unequal country in 1990 to being one of the most unequal countries.
- Income inequality in China today is among the highest in the world.

Government responses to inequality

Income

Personal income tax reform

- To reduce rising inequality, the government raised the minimum threshold for personal income tax in order to reduce the number of people paying tax.
- However, research has found that the redistributive effect of the personal income tax is very limited and ineffective at reducing income inequality.

Minimum wage

- Income inequality was reduced because the average ratio of minimum wage to average wage had increased in the non-private sector and the private sector.
- While minimum wage regulations have reduced wage inequality, the reduction has been very limited because, as earnings increased, tax and welfare policies reduced its effects.

The Dibao system

- This guaranteed a minimum income for employees.
- It covered 45.8 million rural residents (7.8 per cent of the total rural population).
- It gave another 4.97 million rural residents relief assistance for extreme poverty.
- In comparison, 14.9 million urban residents (approximately 1.9 per cent of the urban population) participated in the programme.
- Although it has been effective in alleviating poverty, it did not have a significant impact on reducing income inequality.

Pro-farmer policies

- These are aimed at reducing urban–rural income gaps.
- They are effective as they increase farmers' incomes and reduce the income gaps between urban and rural areas.
- Poverty alleviation policies have also helped to reduce poverty rates.

Health

- China has introduced the following measures to tackle health inequality:
  - ☐ social security
  - ☐ New Rural Cooperative Medical Scheme
  - ☐ Medicare
  - ☐ urban basic pension programme
  - ☐ basic pension insurance programme
- This expansion in medical care coverage is aimed at achieving near-universal coverage for rural residents.
- 378 million people have been helped by the urban basic pension programme.
- Another 508 million people participated in the basic pension insurance programme for urban and rural residents.
- However, due to differences in breadth and depth of coverage among different groups, it is not clear to what extent the advances in the social security system have narrowed inequality.

Education

- China has developed its education system:
  - ☐ 3-year preschool and senior high school education have been made universally available
  - ☐ special support has been given to central and western regions as well as rural or poverty-stricken areas
  - ☐ equal access has been given to compulsory education at local schools for the children of migrant workers
- Overall, this has improved the education system for 'left-behind' children.

Education Law

- Education Law of the People's Republic of China established equal access to enrolment, degrees, and study-abroad programmes.
- These measures have contributed to a rise in the literacy rate of women, from 86.5 per cent in 2000 to 95 per cent in 2019.

Do you know?

1 Give three government responses in the USA **or** China to socio-economic inequality.

2 Give two US Government **or** Chinese Government responses to economic inequality.

3 Name one way in which the US Government **or** Chinese Government responds to educational inequality.

3.5 International influence

You need to know
■ how influential your chosen world power is on the world stage

USA

■ In terms of international influence, the USA:
  □ has a leading role as a permanent member of the UN Security Council
  □ has a leading role in NATO
  □ is a member of the G8
  □ has the largest economy in the world
  □ is a nuclear superpower
  □ has an economic, social and cultural impact on its immediate neighbours, such as Mexico and Canada and on North/Central America as a whole, including Cuba

People's Republic of China

■ In terms of international influence, China:
  □ has a leading role as a permanent member of the UN Security Council
  □ participates in UN peacekeeping operations
  □ has a relationship with and a future role in negotiations with North Korea
  □ has influence due to the impact of US/Chinese diplomatic relations
  □ makes investment in African countries and elsewhere
  □ has growing importance in the world economy (second largest only to the USA, who it is expected to surpass)
  □ is a member of the G20
  □ is part of the G8's Outreach Five (O5)
  □ has an economic, social and cultural impact on its immediate neighbours, such as India, North Korea and on Asia as a whole

Do you know?

1 Give four ways in which the USA **or** China can have international influence.

End of section 3 questions

Option 1

USA

1 Outline the opportunities and limits that exist for people to influence government decision making in the USA.

2 Explain what is meant by the 'separation of powers' and 'checks and balances' in the USA.

3 Outline the socio-economic impact of inequality on groups in the USA.

4 Outline how effective the US Government is at responding to economic inequality.

5 Outline how effective the US Government is at responding to education inequality.

6 Outline how effective the US Government is at responding to employment inequality.

China

1 Outline the opportunities and limits that exist for people to influence government decision making in China.

2 Explain the party system in China.

3 Outline the socio-economic impact of inequality on groups in China.

4 Explain the inequality that exists in China regarding access to drinking water and good sanitation.

5 Outline the health inequality that exists in China between urban and rural dwellers.

6 Outline how effective the Dibao system is at tackling income inequality in China.

7 Outline how effective the Chinese Government is at responding to education inequality.

Option 2 World issues

3.6 Social, economic and political causes

You need to know
■ the social, economic and political factors that have caused the issue you have chosen

Terrorism

Causes of terrorism

Social factors

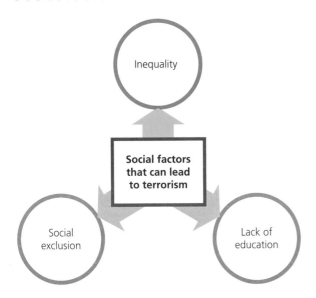

Exam tip

For questions on this topic, you can refer to any significant recent issue or conflict which extends beyond the boundaries of any single country and has an impact which may be regional or global.

- Inequality can cause resentment and frustration from feelings of being ignored and socially excluded with no hope.
- As a result, some people turn to extreme measures (like terrorism) for change and improvement in order to have their voices heard and to express their outrage.
- Lack of education can make some susceptible to **radicalisation** but even highly educated people, if they cannot find employment, may seek solace in extremist ideologies.

Key term

Radicalisation According to the UK Government, radicalisation refers to the process by which a person comes to support terrorism and extremist ideologies associated with terrorist groups.

Example: Tunisia

- In Tunisia there is high unemployment, low educational attainment and many available jobs are low paid and unskilled.
- A number of Tunisians have joined ISIL (Islamic State of Iraq and the Levant, also known as Daesh).
- Terrorists can also be rich and well educated. Karim Cheurfi (also known as Abu Yusuf al-Baljiki), a gunman in the Paris attacks in 2017, was highly educated in politics and fluent in several languages.

Economic factors

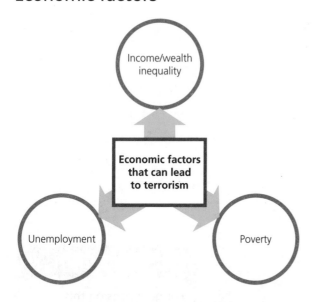

- Inequality and poverty can cause anger and lead to some turning to terrorists for help, seeing it as a way to fight back.
- Income and wealth inequality, linked to unemployment and poverty, can create a situation that suits the recruitment of terrorists.

Example: Belgium

- The children of immigrants in Belgium are 64 per cent more likely to be unemployed than those born in Belgium, which has led to feelings of resentment.
- Of the Europeans who leave their country to join ISIL, many are from Belgium.
- But one in nine people in the world do not have enough to eat and over a billion people live on less than $1 a day – not all of them become terrorists.
- Similarly, many foreign fighters for ISIL are from countries which do not have high levels of poverty and inequality.
- Many women join terrorist groups like ISIL. Around 20 per cent of foreign terrorist fighters are women.

Exam tip

In the exam, evaluation marks will be gained where you make judgements based on criteria, draw conclusions on the extent to which a view is supported by the evidence, provide counter-arguments including possible alternative interpretations, state the overall impact/ significance of the factors when taken together, and show the relative importance of factors in relation to the context.

Political factors

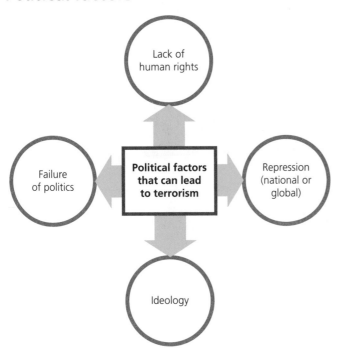

- When a state lacks adequate human rights, people may turn to terrorism to get their own way.
- Terrorist groups seem to help people fight against repression either in their own country or in other countries, resulting in terrorism at a national and international level.
- Some terrorists do not seek violence, but want to exploit their political or ideological goals, such as nationalism.
- Some states have used terrorists to achieve their goals and will sponsor terrorist groups when their goals are similar.

Examples

- Many terrorists say a lack of human rights and lack of trust in their government and police caused them to become radicalised.
- Two-thirds of al-Shabaab (an Islamist militant group) members said they joined because of the Kenyan Government's policies.
  - Thousands of Kenyans have joined al-Shabaab because of high levels of youth unemployment, poverty and hopelessness.
  - Many women have also joined because they experience the highest unemployment rates.
- It is alleged that the attempted assassinations of Sergei and Yulia Skripal in Salisbury, England, is evidence of the Russian state sponsoring terrorists.
- In 1988, 270 people died when terrorists exploded a bomb aboard Pan Am flight 103, allegedly in response to global repression when the USA and Britain bombed Libya. This event is known as the Lockerbie bombing, after the town where the aircraft came down.

Religious factors

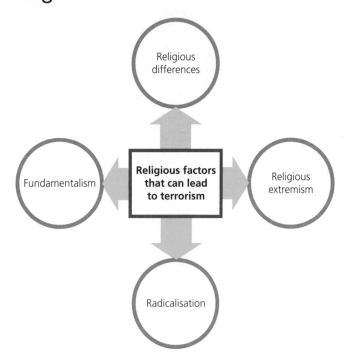

- Religious differences can cause terrorists to punish what is seen as 'ungodly' behaviour, or take revenge for perceived attacks on their beliefs.
- Some fundamentalists and extremists who have been radicalised and are involved in religious terrorism believe that what they do will be forgiven and rewarded in the afterlife.
- Radicalisation can also be promoted through family relationships.

Examples

- Deaths from terrorism rose by 60 per cent between 2015 and 2016, most caused by ISIS and al-Qaeda, both of which have strong religious agendas.
- This implies that religious extremism could be a major cause of terrorism; recently, this has been associated with Islamic fundamentalism.
- 500 former members of extremist groups in Africa said they joined because they felt their religion was being supressed.
- 97 per cent of al-Shabaab members said their religion was under either physical or ideological threat.
- But only a quarter of al-Shabaab members said that religious differences were a problem; instead almost half claimed that the government was their enemy.

Key term

ISIS Islamic State of Iraq and Syria.

Terrorist ideology

- ISIL and al-Qaeda have a common **ideology**.
- Both groups reject democracy, personal liberty and **human rights**, and are committed to restoring a self-proclaimed **Caliphate** and establishing **Sharia law**.
- They hold the West responsible for the suppression of Islam and oppression of Sunni Muslims around the world.
- ISIL and al-Qaeda have used the conflict in Syria and the wider humanitarian crisis to fuel a sense of injustice and ongoing religious conflict between the West and Sunni Islam.

Summary

- When people are dissatisfied with the state of their lives, they are more likely to turn to extreme measures or are more likely to be persuaded to do so.
- Terrorist groups recruit weaker and poorer individuals as they are easier to manipulate and have very little to lose.
- ISIL has persuaded thousands of people, including women and families, to travel to Syria from around the world to join their cause.
- A growing sense of anger and frustration can lead to further radicalisation.

> ## Key terms
>
> **Ideology** The ideas and thoughts that influence a person to act.
>
> **Human rights** The basic rights and freedoms to which all people are entitled.
>
> **Caliphate** An Islamic state under the rule of an Islamic leader.
>
> **Sharia law** Islamic law.

Development in Africa
Contributing factors to underdevelopment

Economic factors

- **Debt:**
    - The total debt burden for African countries is in excess of £200 billion, with annual debt repayments of £14 billion.
    - With some African countries spending billions repaying their debts, they have less to spend on basic social infrastructure such as schools and hospitals.
    - It is estimated that Zambia has a foreign debt of around £10 billion.
    - International Monetary Fund (IMF) conditions of lending make it difficult to ever get out of debt.
- **Trade:**
    - Being rich in natural resources, Africa should be a consistently prosperous continent with many products available to trade and sell to the rest of the world.

> ## Exam tip
>
> You must be able to show the links between different factors. For example, when studying the impact and effects of different factors on development in Africa, you will gain marks by showing that many of the factors are linked and can affect each other.

- ☐ If African countries could earn more through trade, countries would be able to rely less on foreign aid and loans.
- ☐ Trade varies greatly from country to country. Sudan and Nigeria have large oil reserves and can export millions of barrels per day, whereas countries like Malawi and Ethiopia depend heavily on growing and exporting **cash crops** like tea and coffee.
- **Cash crops:**
  - ☐ When they are used to repay debt, farmers/countries can suffer due to market fluctuations and oversupply.
  - ☐ Buyers from developed nations can force down the price of cash crops and therefore reduce the finance flowing into African countries.
- **Lack of infrastructure** is also a huge problem for many African nations and the transportation of goods is not always easy. This severely hinders trade between some African countries.

Political factors

- **Armed conflict:**
  - ☐ This affects crop cultivation and trade supply routes.
  - ☐ It also diverts cash to pay for the conflict.
  - ☐ Oxfam reported that the financial impact of armed conflict in some African countries over a 15-year period was nearly £300 billion.
  - ☐ This led to, on average, 50 per cent more infant deaths, a 5-year reduction in life expectancy and an increase in adult illiteracy.
  - ☐ Armed conflict creates refugees who go without food, water, shelter and medical aid.
  - ☐ Emergency aid can be hampered due to armed conflict, and food production can fall.
  - ☐ Over the last few decades, many African nations have been locked in civil war. In many cases civil war rages for decades and it can take a country years to recover and reconstruct after the conflict has ceased.
- **Bad governance and kleptocracy:**
  - ☐ A major factor that has hindered development in some African countries is the lack of fair and transparent governance.
  - ☐ Bad governance means that taxes will not be collected and therefore cannot be spent on key services that are vital for public use, such as schools and hospitals.
  - ☐ Institutions such as the police, the military and the legal system may not operate in a just and impartial manner, compromising people's human rights.
  - ☐ Corruption has also been a huge problem in the politics of some African countries.

Key term

Cash crop A crop grown to be sold for profit, rather than to be used as food for the grower.

Exam tip

If you make more evaluative or analytical points than are required to gain the maximum allocation of marks, they can be credited as knowledge and understanding marks, provided they meet the criteria for this.

Key term

Kleptocracy Theft of a country's money or resources by the country's ruler.

- ☐ Lack of democracy has allowed many dictators to remain in power for decades, enjoying lavish lifestyles while the population starves.
- ☐ It is estimated that corruption costs the continent around $150 billion a year, with Somalia perceived to be the most corrupt nation on Earth.
- ☐ In Nigeria, up to $9 billion was stolen by its dictator and former governors, ministers and government workers.

Social factors

- **HIV/AIDS:**
  - ☐ Over 20 million Africans have HIV/AIDS, with 1.5 million people dying each year.
  - ☐ The virus mostly affects younger people, with half of those infected being under 25.
  - ☐ HIV/AIDS places a huge cost on countries. Hospitals and health services cannot cope with the epidemic.
  - ☐ The disease reduces life expectancy by up to 20 years and in some countries over 30 per cent of the population are infected.
- **Malaria:**
  - ☐ It is estimated that tackling malaria costs £12 billion per year.
  - ☐ The World Health Organization (WHO) estimates that malaria accounts for up to 50 per cent of hospital admissions.
  - ☐ It kills more than 1 million people each year in sub-Saharan Africa, with 75 per cent of those deaths occurring in children under 5 years.
  - ☐ It is estimated that a child dies every 45 seconds from the disease.
- **Poor educational attainment:**
  - ☐ This holds back development, and debt repayment has affected educational provision because free education is no longer being provided in many African countries.
  - ☐ The average school enrolment in African countries is the lowest in the world, with 33 million children not attending primary school.
  - ☐ When pupils do attend school, they are faced with a lack of basic facilities and resources as well as class sizes of up to 60 pupils.
  - ☐ The level of debt owed by African countries means that they cannot afford to spend money on providing free education.
  - ☐ It is estimated that, due to a lack of finance, secondary education can only be offered to 36 per cent of children in sub-Saharan Africa.

- **'Brain drain':**
  - ☐ The emigration of skilled workers results in a depletion of skilled workers in many African countries.
  - ☐ Around 70,000 skilled professionals emigrate from Africa every year.
  - ☐ Every year, around 12 million young Africans enter the labour market looking for jobs, but only about 3 million jobs are created each year. Many young Africans migrate to Europe and America for jobs.
  - ☐ Half of all Nigeria's doctors are practising abroad.

Economic impact of HIV/AIDS

- HIV/AIDS has meant:
  - ☐ fewer workers are available; the economically active population is reduced
  - ☐ a gender imbalance in the labour force – a reduction in male participation rates and an increase in female participation, suggesting that young widows are looking for work
  - ☐ an age imbalance in the labour force – the biggest increase is in those aged 15–24, suggesting that many young people are looking for work in place of sick or dead older relatives
  - ☐ children/young people leave school early to find work so educational attainment is reduced
  - ☐ skilled and experienced workers who are too ill to work or have died are being replaced by young inexperienced workers

---

Do you know?

1 Give three social factors that have caused terrorism **or** have led to underdevelopment in Africa.

2 Give three economic factors that have caused terrorism **or** have led to underdevelopment in Africa.

3 Give three political factors that have caused terrorism **or** have led to underdevelopment in Africa.

4 Answer **a** or **b**.

   a Give three religious factors that have resulted in terrorism.

   b Give three consequences of HIV/AIDS on the economy of African countries.

3.7 Effects on individuals, families and communities

You need to know
■ the effects of the issue you have chosen on individuals, families and communities

Terrorism
Effects on individuals and families

■ Individuals and families who are victims of terrorism can suffer a multitude of ill-effects as a result, including:
  □ psychological effects (such as post-traumatic stress disorder (PTSD), anxiety, stress, trauma, sleeping disorders)
  □ social effects (such as fear of going outside, or perhaps because of the death of friends or family)
  □ financial effects (for example, if the main earner of a family is injured or killed, there may be difficulties paying bills or affording treatment)
  □ health effects (such as injury, possibly resulting in physical disability)
■ Survivors of terrorist attacks often experience psychological problems, with around half suffering from PTSD and depression.
■ Many also turn to alcohol and drugs, some to excess, with high levels of anxiety around visiting places where attacks happened or where there are many people in one area, for example, using public transport or visiting shopping centres.

Exam tip

In the exam, you will gain marks if you can refer to the nature of your chosen issue and its impact on individuals, families and communities (such as poverty, ill health and lower educational attainment) and on your ability to evaluate the relative severity of the impact of the issue.

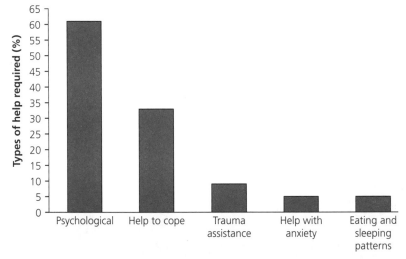

Figure 3.4 Needs of victims and their families following a terrorist attack

Answers at **www.hoddereducation.co.uk/needtoknow/answers**

Example

Manchester Arena bombing

■ The singer Ariana Grande suffered from PTSD following the Manchester Arena terror attack in May 2017.

■ After what they experienced and saw at the concert, some witnesses suffered from depression and had to take antidepressants.

■ Some witnesses also had nightmares and difficulty sleeping.

■ 22 people lost their lives as a result of the attack and 120 people were injured.

■ Some surviving victims lost limbs and had to have operations for their injuries. For example, one had to have fingers stitched back onto their hands and pieces of metal removed from their body.

■ Some victims were left with scars, most notably on their faces, which some admitted to trying to cover up when with friends. This has affected them psychologically and led to PTSD.

Effects on communities

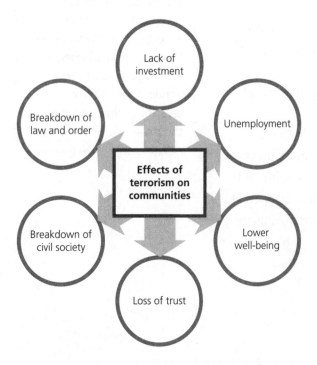

■ Attacks on businesses, cities and countries can cost them £ billions and lead to closures and unemployment.

■ Terror attacks in 2017 cost the UK economy £3 billion.

■ The UK suffered the biggest economic loss (£40 billion) from terrorism among all EU countries between 2005 and 2017.

Table 3.5 Cost of terrorism in 2017 by country

Country	Cost of terrorism (£ billion)
UK	45
France	43
Spain	41
EU	180

- Investment and spending drops as a result.
- After terror attacks, some people begin to mistrust others and seek revenge, which can lead to a breakdown of law and order.
- However, the negative economic effects tend to be short-lived and there is evidence that they only apply within the year of the incident.

Examples

- Tourists may avoid places which were attacked, causing economic losses (as was the case after the gun attack in Tunisia in June 2015) but after a few months things usually get back to normal.
- Manchester hotels experienced a fall in occupancy the day after the attack but began to get back to normal after a few days.
- **Hate crime:**
  - ☐ In the UK, Islamophobic hate crime incidents significantly increased between 2014 and 2017.
  - ☐ In the week after the Manchester bombing there were 139 Islamophobic attacks compared to 25 the week before.
  - ☐ In Scotland, Islamophobic incidents rose by 89 per cent between 2015 and 2016.

Annual date	Number of Islamophobic hate crime incidents in the UK
June 2017	1,535
June 2016	1,227
June 2015	807
June 2014	520

Backlash of terrorist attacks in the UK

- After the attack on Westminster Bridge in March 2017:
  - ☐ members of the public verbally abused a Muslim student with taunts such as 'Muslims are the only terrorists' and 'they only seem to be attacking us'
  - ☐ others approached a Muslim woman on a bus who was wearing Islamic clothing, asking if she was 'carrying a bomb', pointing at her hijab and saying, 'People like you were responsible for the Westminster Bridge attack', and then spitting on her hijab

- After the Manchester Arena bombing in May 2017:
  - ☐ a group of school pupils singled out a teenage Muslim girl, threatening her for being Muslim and shouting 'ISIS' at her
  - ☐ others questioned her about her whereabouts at the time of the Manchester attack
- The day after the London Bridge attack in June 2017, a fake bomb was placed outside Paisley Central Mosque carrying the message 'Youse are next, defo.'

Development in Africa
Effects of underdevelopment on individuals, families and communities

- Underdevelopment can lead to poverty, lack of education and poor health, causing suffering for individuals, families and communities, and lead to conflict and social unrest.
- Today in many places in Africa, bacteria are growing increasingly resistant to antibiotics, so disease (including new diseases such as avian flu and SARS) is an increasing problem.
- In African countries, especially east and southern Africa, HIV/AIDS is a major health issue. Other major health issues include malaria and tuberculosis.
- All of these issues are compounded by starvation and hunger, lack of access to clean water and sanitation, which also increases the spread of disease.

HIV/AIDS in east and southern Africa

- This is the most affected region in the world and is home to the largest number of people living with HIV.
- This region is occupied by 6.2 per cent of the world's population.
- This region also contains over half of the total number of people living with HIV in the world (19.6 million people).
- Half a million people died of AIDS-related illnesses in 2016 in this region.
- 66 per cent of adults and 59 per cent of children are on antiretroviral drugs.
- The main route for HIV transmission among children is through birth.
- The number of young women aged 15–24 years with HIV is double that of young men (3.4 per cent compared to 1.6 per cent).

Effects on children

- Children in underdeveloped areas are more likely to be malnourished than adults.
- Poor nutrition plays a role in around half of all child deaths in Africa.
- Five children aged under 5 years die every minute in the African region, two-thirds of them from preventable causes.
- Diarrhoeal and respiratory infections, malaria, measles and malnutrition represent big threats to child health.
- Pneumonia and malaria are the leading causes of death among children under 5 years of age.
- The interaction of undernourishment and infection can lead to a vicious cycle of worsening illness and deteriorating nutritional status.

Child soldiers

- As a direct result of armed conflict, many vulnerable children are caught up in war.
- In several countries in Africa, children are being forced to take part in wars, fighting as child soldiers.
- The number of children used in armed conflicts around the world has more than doubled since 2012, with a 159 per cent rise.
- It is estimated that there are 250,000 child soldiers in the world, with 60 per cent of those in Africa.
- Currently, child soldiers are being used in armed conflicts in the Central African Republic, Chad, the Democratic Republic of Congo, Mali, Somalia and Sudan.
- The psychological effects on children are felt long after they are finished fighting.

- Many child soldiers are used as fighters and at checkpoints, as informants, to loot villages and as domestic and sexual slaves. They become desensitised to violence and they see and do things that can leave lasting mental scars.
- Furthermore, most child soldiers will have missed out on school and without an education they have very poor future prospects.

Effects on families

Famine and malnutrition

- Famine is caused by the shortage of or inability of people to obtain food.
- This might be caused by low food production resulting from drought or other factors, such as armed conflict or bad governance.
- Around one-third of all people who live in sub-Saharan Africa are undernourished.
- An estimated 275 million people in Africa each day go hungry.
- Children are the most visible victims of malnutrition. Children who are poorly nourished suffer up to 160 days of illness each year.
- Poor nutrition plays a role in around half of all child deaths on average in Africa.
- Malnutrition magnifies the effect of every disease, including measles and malaria, and can contribute to low life expectancy, infant deaths, long term effects on ability to work and loss of earnings.

Corruption

- Individuals and families are affected by corruption in some African countries, with half the population reporting that they have to pay a bribe to stop their family homes from being taken away.

Effects on girls

- Most girls cannot afford to attend school.
- An estimated 31 million girls of primary school age and 32 million girls of lower-secondary school age were out of school in 2013.
- Girls associated with armed groups and forces totalled 893 in 2018, four times more than the 216 recorded in 2017.

Lack of educated workforce

- Lack of education results in a low-skilled and low-educated workforce.
- High rates of adult illiteracy lead to low-paid jobs and unemployment, which in turn leads to economic underdevelopment.

- A low government revenue impacts on the future development of communities, so conditions cannot improve.

Effects on farmers

- Investment in cash crops that depend heavily on the export market is widespread.
- Farmers lease land to foreign companies to grow their own cash crops, creating a dependency on them for many farmers and families.

Lack of social services

- Debt and trade issues mean that many African countries lack the type of social services we are accustomed to in Scotland.
- Social services are very important, as without an adequate education and health system, any country will fail to prosper.
- Schools often lack basic amenities such as electricity and running water.
- Hospitals are underfunded and under-resourced with too few doctors and nurses.
- Many people living in rural areas have no education or health facilities at all.
- Angola's debt highlights the problem, where 44 per cent of government revenue is spent on repaying external debt and only 6 per cent is spent on public health.
- A skilled, educated and healthy workforce is required for a country to move towards development.

Do you know?

1 List the effects of terrorism **or** underdevelopment in Africa on individuals and families.
2 Give three effects that terrorism has on communities **or** that HIV/AIDS has in Africa.
3 Answer **a** or **b**.
  a Which country in the EU has faced the highest cost in monetary terms from terrorism?
  b Which region in Africa is the most affected by HIV and is home to the largest number of people living with HIV in the world?

3.8 Effects on governments and the international community

You need to know

- how to analyse the effects of the world issue you have chosen on countries and their governments

Terrorism

- Terrorism can have a wide range of effects on countries and their governments.
- On top of fatalities and serious and life-changing injuries for the victims, it can also have major economic effects, with businesses, cities and nations losing billions in the aftermath of attacks.
- In addition, emotional and psychological trauma from injuries and deaths affect individuals, families, communities and nations.

Table 3.6 Terrorist incidents in selected countries (2017)

Country	No. of incidents
Iraq	2,466
Afghanistan	1,414
Pakistan	719
India	692
Somalia	614
UK	122
Colombia	117
USA	65
France	41
Russia	33
Germany	27
Canada	12

Table 3.7 Fatalities from terrorist attacks in selected countries (2017)

Country	No. of fatalities
World total	26,445
Iraq	6,476
Afghanistan	6,092
Syria	2,026
USA	95
UK	36

Table 3.8 Fatalities from terrorist attacks in EU countries (2017)

EU country	No. of fatalities
EU total	Over 800
UK	36
Spain	16
Sweden	5
France	3
Finland	2
Germany	1

- There were more fatalities from terrorist attacks in the UK in 2017 than in any other EU country.
- In the UK, all of these fatalities were caused by ISIS-inspired attacks in Westminster, Manchester, London Bridge and Finsbury Park.

Effects on countries

Trade

- Terrorism can increase the costs of doing business with countries that have been attacked or are under the threat of attack.
- This can lead to an increase in the price of products and cause a reduction of exports and imports.
- For example, transport costs will rise if traders have to pay high or inflated insurance to cover potential claims for damage or loss when transporting goods into countries that have been or could be affected by terrorism.
- These costs can be passed on to consumers through higher product prices.

Growth and direct foreign investment

- For developing countries, growth and development can be hindered.
- Terrorism can affect bilateral aid between donor countries and those under threat from terrorism.
- It can also make it difficult for countries to attract direct foreign investment.

Effects on the international community

- Terrorism is a barrier to economic growth.
  - ☐ The 28 EU member states lost over £200 billion in GDP terms due to terrorism between 2004 and 2017.
  - ☐ Terror attacks in 2017 cost the UK economy £3 billion.
  - ☐ The UK suffered the biggest economic loss (£40 billion) from terrorism out of all EU countries between 2005 and 2017.
- Terrorism results in an increase in psychological issues, even for those not directly involved in attacks.
- Governments and individuals can alter their behaviours. Governments may become more cautious and suspicious of citizens while citizens seek happiness by living in the moment, consuming more and saving and investing less.
- Terrorism results in a reduction in tourism and less income for governments from the tourist trade.
- It leads to increased healthcare costs.
- It causes an increase in property damage and repair costs.
- Terrorism also reduces health and well-being among citizens who are involved directly and indirectly.
- Finally, it can reduce citizens' trust in governments, the legal system and the police.

Development in Africa

Effects on African governments

- Lack of development causes:
  - ☐ economic problems for African countries
  - ☐ greater social problems, leading to greater need for government spending
  - ☐ reliance on outside aid

Economic effects of underdevelopment

- There is heavy investment in cash crops to try to pay off debts (which proves ineffective).
- There is a lack of infrastructure:
  - ☐ This impacts education and health (too few schools and hospitals in some areas).
  - ☐ Lack of good roads can make it difficult to transport goods, resulting in a loss of potential trade.
- There are high levels of debt:
  - ☐ Nearly half of all African countries are facing a major debt crisis.
  - ☐ Eight African countries are currently in **debt distress** and 18 more are at high risk of joining them.
  - ☐ This number has more than doubled since 2013.

> **Key term**
>
> **Debt distress** Difficulties caused by increasing debts and lack of money.

- Widespread lack of development is compounded by corruption in some places that pushes potential investors away.
- On average, around one-quarter of all development funds are stolen or go missing each year in Africa.
- Mass unemployment results in lower revenue for the country.
- External dependency is created, caused by over-reliance on foreign companies, foreign governments and aid.

Social effects of underdevelopment

- **Weak education systems:** Education can help break the cycle of poverty but it is a long-term investment that the governments cannot afford.
- **Poor healthcare systems:** There is a lack of universal healthcare to educate people in the prevention and treatment of illness, for example, HIV/AIDs, Ebola.
- Countries are unable to afford to invest in healthcare and education, holding back future development.
- Food insecurity is rife, especially in areas where cash crops are grown instead of food.
- Poverty is widespread, often as a result of little education, poor nutrition and few job opportunities.
- There is a lack of adequate sanitation facilities as countries cannot afford to pay for them, which can aid the spread of disease.
- Gender discrimination can occur. Cultural health disparity can become more prominent with services more suited to males than females. For example, gender-biased services can neglect women's health needs such as birth control, pregnancy and childbirth. Also, women often must make the choice between sending their child to school, purchasing food or paying for a health visit.

Effects of underdevelopment on the wider international community

- Some African countries cannot pay back their debt.
  - ☐ This presents significant risks for the wider international community's commitments to end extreme poverty.
  - ☐ Bad management of this debt crisis is setting back progress towards the Sustainable Development Goals and reversing the development progress already made.

- Government corruption in African countries has implications for the wider international community:
  - ☐ Corruption continues to prevent development in some countries in Africa.
  - ☐ It prevents democracy, development and the ability to end poverty.
  - ☐ The African continent ranks lowest among global regions in the **Corruption Perceptions Index (CPI)**.
- The issues of famine and starvation have had an impact on the wider international community who have had to send aid.
- Many countries have been forced to take action to prevent corruption and the abuse of human rights.
- Dealing with civil wars:
  - ☐ Civil war in South Sudan has led to 400,000 deaths. Sixty per cent of the population are on the verge of famine, almost 2 million of its 12 million population are internally displaced and a further 2 million have fled to neighbouring nations, e.g. Uganda.
  - ☐ The international community is trying to bring about a peace agreement with the United Nations Security Council hoping to put in place a resolution renewing a former mandate of the UN Mission in South Sudan (UNMISS) to address sexual violence, and to help internally displaced people to return home.

Key term

Corruption Perceptions Index (CPI) This rates countries on how corrupt their governments are believed to be.

Do you know?

If your chosen world issue is terrorism...

1 What are the wide range of effects that terrorism can have on countries and their governments?
2 Which country had the highest number of terrorist incidents around the world in 2017?
3 Which country had the highest number of fatalities from terrorist attacks in 2017?
4 Which country had the highest number of fatalities from terrorist attacks in EU countries in 2017?
5 Give two effects of terrorism on countries.
6 Give two effects of terrorism on the wider international community.

If your chosen world issue is development in Africa...

1 Give two effects which underdevelopment has had on Africa and African governments.
2 What are two economic problems faced by African countries as a result of underdevelopment?
3 What are two social problems faced by African countries as a result of underdevelopment?
4 Give three problems for the wider international community that have resulted from underdevelopment in Africa.

3.9 Effectiveness of responses by individual countries

You need to know

■ the effectiveness of the affected countries in tackling the issue you have chosen, for example, the effectiveness of the UK in tackling terrorism or the effectiveness of the UK in tackling a lack of development in Africa

Terrorism

UK strategies to tackle international terrorism

Government strategy	Effectiveness
Military: ■ The UK is assisting the Nigerian military to tackle **Boko Haram**, who pledge allegiance to ISIS ■ It is also training and equipping Kurdish **Peshmerga** to fight ISIS ■ It has also used air strikes to disrupt ISIS positions	Boko Haram has been forced out of almost all of the areas that it controlled in north-east Nigeria
Humanitarian: ■ **DFID** is involved in carrying out the UK's humanitarian strategy to help end the conflict in Syria, which is a magnet and safe haven for the training of British and foreign terrorists ■ DFID has provided over 22 million food rations, over 9 million medical consultations, and over 5 million vaccines since 2012	■ Almost 5 million people in Syria have been provided with sustainable access to clean water and/or sanitation ■ Around 200,000 Syrian children have been helped to return to school and gain a decent education ■ 350,000 women and children have been lifted out of poverty
Financial: ■ The UK is helping Libya to cope with the threat of terrorist groups and the growing problems of refugees and displaced people risking their lives trying to cross the Mediterranean ■ It has given £4 million to remove mines planted by ISIS, £1 million for rebuilding damaged buildings, £2.75 million for supporting women's participation in peace-making and £1.3 million for food and healthcare for refugees	■ It is helping to bring some stability to Libya, making it a less attractive area for terrorists, gun-runners and people traffickers ■ ISIS has been pushed back and landmines have been cleared ■ But, due to the country's unstable situation, the money provided is not being spent as intended but is being siphoned off by corrupt groups

Key terms

Boko Haram Means 'Western education is forbidden'. It is a militant Islamic group in Nigeria that wants to create an Islamic State with Sharia law.

Peshmerga Means 'Those who face death'. These are Kurdish fighters in northern Iraq fighting ISIS.

DFID The Department for International Development — the UK government department responsible for administering overseas aid with the aim of promoting sustainable development and eliminating world poverty.

CONTEST

- The purpose of CONTEST (the UK's counter-terrorism strategy) is to reduce the risk of terrorism to the UK, its people and international interests, so that people can live their lives safely and freely.
- The strategic framework consists of the 'four Ps':
  - ☐ **Prevent:** to stop people becoming terrorists or supporting terrorism.
  - ☐ **Pursue:** to stop terrorist attacks.
  - ☐ **Protect:** to strengthen our protection against a terrorist attack.
  - ☐ **Prepare:** to mitigate the impact of a terrorist attack.
- So far, the strategy has been effective, evidenced by the police and security services intercepting 25 Islamist terror plots between 2013 and 2018, including four extreme right-wing terror plots in 2018.
- However, the racial equality organisation, JUST Yorkshire, say CONTEST is ineffective because it focuses on Islamophobia and racism.

UK strategies to tackle national terrorism

Government strategy	Description
Counter-terrorism strategy	Deals with terrorism within UK and has disrupted financial supply networks and ISIS volunteers leaving the UK to join ISIS in Syria The Office for Security and Counter-Terrorism and the Treasury are jointly responsible for the UK's Counter Terrorist Finance Strategy
The Terrorism Asset-Freezing Act and Al-Qaeda Asset-Freezing Regulations	Have enabled police forces to freeze the bank accounts of those suspected of being involved in terrorism
Community work schemes	Aim to prevent extremism and radicalisation in areas of high Muslim populations in the UK

Development in Africa
UK responses by DFID

Government (DFID) strategy	Effectiveness
Humanitarian	Effective because life-saving humanitarian aid has been provided to: ■ over 1.5 million people in the Sahel region who are affected by food insecurity and conflict ■ almost 2 million people to cope with the effect of climate change and other natural disasters Ineffective because: ■ more work is required to help 3 million people avoid the worst effects of drought in the Sahel region ■ more work is needed to support up to 3 million people with food assistance in the Sahel region
Economic development	Effective because: ■ DFID's work on improving cross-border trade, access to electricity and agricultural productivity is helping to reduce barriers to economic growth in Africa ■ by reducing trade barriers in east Africa, DFID has helped to reduce freight costs from Uganda to Kenya by 35 per cent ■ DFID is supporting agriculture to improve incomes for around 5 million people in Africa and is encouraging new private investment Ineffective because: ■ more work is required to help 3.2 million people get access to household electricity for the first time
Basic services	Effective because DFID is: ■ providing basic family planning services to around 4 million additional women and girls ■ supporting African countries to prevent and tackle deadly diseases including malaria and Ebola ■ securing sustainable access to clean water and/or sanitation to over 700,000 people Ineffective because: ■ more work is required to end female genital mutilation
Overall	Effective because the UK (through DFID) is: ■ helping to create a more stable and prosperous Africa which is good for both Africa and the UK ■ providing diplomatic and financial investment which is helping to grow Africa's economy in terms of trade and investment ■ supporting Africa's ability to solve its own problems, e.g. humanitarian crises, conflicts, terrorism and corruption ■ supporting Africa to provide more jobs and greater opportunities for its young workforce, thereby reducing migration to Europe and over-reliance on UK aid

Do you know?

1 List three ways in which the UK has attempted to tackle terrorism **or** has responded to underdevelopment in Africa.

2 Answer **a** or **b**.

   a What is the 'four Ps' strategic framework of CONTEST?

   b What does 'DFID' stand for?

3 Answer **a** or **b**.

   a In what way has CONTEST been effective at dealing with terrorism?

   b In what ways has DFID been effective in responding to underdevelopment in Africa?

4 Why has CONTEST **or** DFID been criticised?

3.10 Effectiveness of responses by international organisations

Exam tip

In the exam, regardless of your chosen world issue, you can gain marks by referring to the nature of the issue and the international organisations involved (such as those above) and analysing the successes and/or shortcomings of the actions of these organisations and the reasons for these successes and/or failures.

You need to know
- how effective an international organisation is in tackling your chosen issue

Terrorism
International strategies to tackle terrorism

- The main aim of the UN Global Counter-Terrorism Strategy is to prevent and combat terrorism.
- Its framework consists of four pillars:
  - Pillar 1: tackling the conditions that help the spread of terrorism
  - Pillar 2: preventing and combatting terrorism
  - Pillar 3: assisting threatened states and strengthening the role of the UN
  - Pillar 4: protecting human rights and the rule of law
- It has been effective because:
  - The UN has supported the Northern Alliance in Afghanistan against the Taliban's threat to the state. In doing so the UN has tackled the conditions that were helping the spread of terrorism and so has been effective in preventing and combating terrorism, protecting the rule of law in the country and protecting the human rights of Afghan citizens.
- It has been ineffective because it has failed to adequately address the human rights abuses, including gender inequalities, while countering terrorism. Research shows a correlation between gender equality and a decrease in violent extremism.
  - By supporting the Afghan Northern Alliance in Afghanistan against the Taliban's threat to the state, state control was given to known warlords.
  - This led to corruption so bad that people turned to terrorism because they saw the Taliban as a better way of solving their problems.

EU strategies to tackle terrorism

- The main aim of the EU counter-terrorism strategy is to fight terrorism globally and make Europe safer.

- The strategic framework consists of:
  - ☐ Prevent: prevent people turning to terrorism
  - ☐ Protect: protect people and infrastructure
  - ☐ Pursue: pursue terrorists throughout the world
  - ☐ Respond: be ready to respond to all types of terrorist attacks
- It has been effective because:
  - ☐ It has reinforced checks at external borders.
  - ☐ It is reducing terrorist propaganda online.
  - ☐ It is taking action to reduce money laundering and terrorist financing.
  - ☐ The EU's European Arrest Warrant (EAW) collects and exchanges information and evidence to bring terrorists to justice.
  - ☐ The EU helps states that are vulnerable to extremism to try to prevent terrorism.
  - ☐ However, in doing so it has supported air strikes that have killed civilians and encouraged communities to turn to extremists as a lesser evil.

NATO strategies to tackle terrorism

- NATO's work on counter-terrorism focuses on:
  - ☐ improving **awareness** of the threat
  - ☐ developing **capabilities** to prepare and respond
  - ☐ enhancing **engagement** with partner countries and other international actors

NATO strategy	Effectiveness
Awareness	Through cooperation with international organisations, NATO has improved awareness of terrorism and shared knowledge of international counter-terrorism efforts
Capabilities	Through the Defence Against Terrorism Programme of Work (DAT POW), NATO has protected armed forces, civilians and infrastructure from terrorist attack, such as suicide bombers, mines, rocket attacks and the use of chemical, biological or radiological material and weapons of mass destruction (WMD)
Engagement	As a member of the Global Coalition to Defeat ISIS, fighting international terrorism, NATO has taught Iraqi security forces how to clear mines in territory previously occupied by ISIL, significantly reducing the number of civilian casualties and deaths

Summary

- The UK, UN, EU, NATO and international organisations have eroded ISIL territory and reduced its ability to launch attacks from Syria and Iraq.
- But ISIL still has many followers, resources and the ability to direct attacks around the world.
- ISIL remains the most significant terrorist threat globally and continues to motivate thousands of people, including women and families, to travel to Syria from around the world to join its cause.

- Despite the death of Osama Bin Laden in September 2012 and its reduced capability, al-Qaeda remains a global threat.
- al-Qaeda retains cells in Afghanistan, the Middle East and Africa as well as strong links with extremist groups in Syria and Iraq.
- The most prominent of these groups is Hayat Tahrir al-Sham (HTS), which is active in the Syrian conflict.

Development in Africa
Types of international aid

- International organisations give aid which can help to tackle lack of development in Africa and help African countries overcome the challenges they face.
- Aid can take various forms, from humanitarian emergency assistance to longer-term development aid.
- It is important that the aid goes towards targeting the specific problems of that nation.
- There are three main types of aid: **bilateral**, **multilateral** and **voluntary**.

Bilateral

- This is aid given from one government to another.
- Developed countries will target specific countries that require aid.
- Britain's bilateral aid is organised by DFID.
- Bilateral aid is considered to be effective because it places conditions and restrictions on the aid that are closely monitored.
- Thus, it is considered to be more sustainable and to ensure cost-effectiveness through greater control over aid funds.
- However, bilateral aid can sometimes be 'tied', reducing its effectiveness and transfer value to the recipient.

Multilateral

- Multilateral aid is given by international organisations such as the EU and the UN.
- It is considered to be more effective than bilateral aid because it is more likely to be allocated based on development considerations.
- Multilateral agencies are viewed as more politically neutral and publicly acceptable, leading to better cooperation with recipient countries.

Voluntary aid

- This is aid given by NGOs or charities.
- Many NGOs (such as Oxfam) fund specialised projects in developing countries, for example, building schools or water pumps.

Ineffective aid?

- Well-intentioned aid can become ineffective when there are no effective mechanisms in place to monitor and make recipients accountable for spending.
- This is exacerbated if corruption is high.
- In addition, there are not enough ways to evaluate the quality of projects funded mainly by international organisations and UN agencies.

Tied aid

- Tied aid is bilateral aid that, when donated, has conditions attached.
- These conditions stipulate that the receiving country has to use the aid to buy goods and services from the donor country.
- In this setup, the donor country is benefiting as well. This type of aid has been criticised as:
  - ☐ it costs up to 30 per cent more than untied aid for goods and services and more for food aid
  - ☐ recipient countries are unable to secure best value for money, goods and services
  - ☐ it raises unfair barriers to open competition for aid-funded buying and selling
  - ☐ if it is used to tackle health issues like malaria, then bad value for money can cost lives.

Responses by international organisations

The UN and its agencies

- The UN operates a series of specialised agencies that aim to deliver multilateral aid and assistance.
- Each agency has a particular focus and remit when it comes to meeting the needs of developing nations.
- The UN has an excellent track record of providing aid.
- However, underfunding and countries cutting back on voluntary contributions has meant restrictions or cancellations of key projects.
- The UN's work is often undermined by corrupt regimes and bad governance.
- Aid can often be misdirected by corrupt regimes.
- Food aid can be seen as a short-term solution which doesn't address long-term causes of the issue.
- Tied aid often favours the donor country rather than the receiving country.

The EU

- The EU is committed to the Cotonou Agreement.
- It has received criticism that the terms of agreement weigh too much in favour of the EU.
- It was criticised for being too slow and inefficient with aid being misspent.
- Its progress towards the Millennium Development Goals has been slow and inconsistent.

The UK

- The UK is committed to spending 0.7 per cent of its GDP on development through DFID, but currently only gives 0.4 per cent.

The African Union (AU)

- Its main aim is to help African countries to run their own affairs.
- It has been criticised for being too bureaucratic and slow to respond to crises.
- It is poorly financed, which limits its scope to achieve its aims.
- In terms of helping the African economy, the AU works to ensure fair trade takes place.
- It also works to prevent and combat corruption.

Effectiveness of responses

UN agencies

UNICEF at work in Africa

- UNICEF works around the world, focusing on improving the lives of children.

> **Key terms**
>
> **Contonou Agreement** An agreement between the EU and the African, Caribbean and Pacific group of states to help development between 2000 and 2020.
>
> **Millennium Development Goals** Global partnership to reduce extreme poverty.
>
> **GDP** Gross domestic product.

- Considering a child dies every 15 seconds in Africa, the job UNICEF does is vital in saving lives in the developing world.
- Since the launch of Schools for Africa, more than 12 million children have benefited from increased access to and quality of education.
- This has included UNICEF building 415 new classrooms in the remotest parts of Mali and Burkina Faso.
- It has also trained 10,000 teachers in Ethiopia, Mali, Malawi, Burkina Faso and Niger.

WHO at work in Africa

- WHO helps to meet the health needs of people by providing information and training about health issues.
- WHO also carries out healthcare itself, such as immunisation campaigns to wipe out killer diseases like tuberculosis.
- WHO is engaged in an initiative to assist the most affected countries in sub-Saharan Africa.
- The initiative aims to improve access to diagnosis and treatment for the major causes of death in children under 5 years of age, namely malaria, pneumonia and diarrhoea.

Non-governmental organisations (NGOs) and charitable groups

Oxfam

- Oxfam aims to help people to lift themselves out of poverty and thrive.
- Oxfam is working in South Sudan to deliver humanitarian aid to people affected by the armed conflict, by providing clean water, hygiene facilities, food, fuel and income support.

The Red Cross

- The International Red Cross and Red Crescent Movement (known as the Red Cross) is a humanitarian organisation that aims to protect human health and life, and prevent human suffering.
- Red Cross volunteers have helped nearly 160,000 people in communities across North Kivu in the Democratic Republic of Congo.
- Here they provide lifesaving information about Ebola.
- They have also carried out over 235 safe and dignified burials which are crucial to reducing the spread of the disease.

Doctors without Borders/Médecins sans Frontières

■ This is an international, independent, medical humanitarian organisation that delivers emergency aid to people affected by armed conflict, epidemics, healthcare exclusion and natural disasters.

■ In 2017, in the Central African Republic, Médecins sans Frontières carried out 748,600 outpatient consultations, treated 444,600 patients for malaria and administered 63,800 measles vaccinations.

Amnesty International

■ This organisation fights abuses of human rights worldwide, helping to bring torturers to justice, change oppressive laws and free people who have been jailed just for voicing their opinion.

■ In 2018, Amnesty International provided credible evidence that the Sudanese Government forces had carried out war crimes and crimes against humanity (including the use of chemical weapons) in the Jebel Marra region of Darfur, Sudan.

■ In 2018 it also highlighted numerous massacres of Muslims in the Central African Republic, and the violent expulsion of the remaining Muslim population from the western half of the country.

■ This led the UN Security Council to send a peacekeeping force to the Central African Republic to protect the civilian population.

Do you know?

If your chosen issue is terrorism…

1 What is the main aim of the UN Global Counter-Terrorism Strategy?
2 What are the four pillars of the UN Global Counter-Terrorism Strategy?
3 What is the aim of the EU counter-terrorism strategy?
4 What does NATO's work on counter-terrorism focus on?

If your chosen issue is development in Africa…

1 What is the main aim of UN agencies in tackling underdevelopment in Africa?
2 Name four UN agencies tackle underdevelopment in Africa?
3 What is the aim of the African Union in relation to tackling underdevelopment in Africa?
4 What does UNICEF's work in Africa focus on?

End of section 3 questions

Option 2

Terrorism

1 Explain the social factors that have caused terrorism.

2 Explain the economic factors that have caused terrorism.

3 Explain the political factors that have caused terrorism.

4 Explain the religious factors that have caused terrorism.

5 Explain the effects of terrorism on victims and their families.

6 Explain the effects of terrorism on communities.

7 Outline the trend in hate crime in the UK in recent years.

8 Outline how effective the UK has been in tackling terrorism.

9 Outline how effective the UN has been in tackling terrorism.

10 Outline how effective the EU has been in tackling terrorism.

11 Outline how effective NATO has been in tackling terrorism.

12 Outline the overall effectiveness of international organisations in tackling terrorism.

Development in Africa

1 Explain the economic, political and social factors that can cause underdevelopment in Africa.

2 Explain the impact of HIV/AIDS on the economy in African countries.

3 Explain the effects of underdevelopment on children in Africa.

4 Outline the issue of child soldiers in Africa.

5 Explain the effects of underdevelopment on families in Africa.

6 Explain the effects of underdevelopment on girls in Africa.

7 Explain the economic effects of underdevelopment in Africa.

8 Explain the social effects of underdevelopment in Africa.

9 Explain the effects on the wider international community of underdevelopment in Africa.

10 Outline how effective DFID has been in responding to underdevelopment in Africa.

11 Outline how effective the UN has been in tackling underdevelopment in Africa.

12 Outline the three main types of aid.

13 Outline the main aims of non-governmental organisations (NGOs) and charitable groups in tackling underdevelopment in Africa.

4 Analysing, evaluating and synthesising

Question Paper 2

The accuracy question

You need to know

■ that this source-based question is worth 10 marks and has 2–4 sources
■ that this question will have the following stem: 'To what extent is it accurate to state that…'
■ how to detect and explain the degree of objectivity in a given view

■ In the exam you can get:
   □ up to 8 marks for using evidence in all the sources to give an accurate evaluation of the view given in the question
   □ up to 3 marks for any one explanation of the extent of objectivity where you use evidence appropriately. This will depend on the quality of your explanation and how you synthesise the evidence
■ For full marks:
   □ you must refer to all the given sources in your answer, otherwise you can only get a maximum of 6 marks
   □ you must make an overall judgement as to the extent of the accuracy and/or objectivity of the given statement in the question. You can get up to a further 2 marks for doing this
■ You must:
   □ include a 'quantitative' judgement, for example, 'largely accurate', and support this with the most convincing evidence from the sources. If you say that the statement is totally accurate or totally inaccurate you will get 0 marks
   □ avoid judgements such as 'accurate to a certain extent' as they are too vague

onclusions question

u need to know

- that this source-based question is worth 10 marks and has 2–4 sources
- that this question will have the following stem: 'What conclusions can be drawn…'
- how to make and support conclusions about points given in the question

- In the exam you can get:
  - □ up to 8 marks for using the evidence in the sources to make evaluative comments or judgement(s) or draw a conclusion about each of the three points given in the question
  - □ up to 3 marks for any one conclusion if you use evidence appropriately, depending on the quality of your explanation and the synthesis of the evidence you use from the sources
  - □ up to a further 2 marks for an overall conclusion
- For full marks:
  - □ you must refer to all sources in your answer, otherwise you can only get a maximum of 6 marks
  - □ you must make and support three conclusions about each of the three points given in the question and make an overall conclusion on the issue
- You must:
  - □ provide developed and insightful conclusions, making evaluative comments, having scrutinised the source material. All of the marks in this question are awarded for using sources and are not awarded for the conclusion itself. However, without a valid conclusion, you will get 0 marks
  - □ interpret and/or evaluate complex sources in order to reach conclusions
  - □ show evidence which explains your conclusions
- You must not:
  - □ provide your overall conclusion as a reworded summary of your answer given for the three bullet points. Although you can use the same evidence, your overall conclusion must provide an evaluative judgement which is relevant to the wording of the question
  - □ use background knowledge as this will gain 0 marks

The reliability question

You need to know

- that this source-based question is worth 8 marks and has 3 sources
- that this question will have the following stem: 'To what extent are sources... reliable.'
- how to evaluate the reliability of a source or explain why sources are or are not reliable

- How to answer this question:
  - ☐ You must state the extent to which the source is or is not reliable.
  - ☐ Then you must give two distinct pieces of evidence from the source to accurately explain why this is so. This will get you 2 marks. You have to do this three times for three separate sources, giving you: $3 \times 2 = 6$ marks.
  - ☐ To finish, you must then give an overall conclusion saying which source is the most reliable of the three and give evidence from the sources explaining why your chosen source is more reliable than both the other two sources.
- You can get:
  - ☐ up to 6 marks for an accurate evaluation of source reliability
  - ☐ a further 2 marks for an overall judgement on the most reliable source
  - ☐ up to 2 marks for any one explanation of the extent of reliability if you use evidence appropriately. This depends on the quality of your explanation and the synthesis of the evidence you provide
  - ☐ a maximum of 3 marks if you only consider one factor, for example, date, bias, sample size, provenance
- For full marks you must:
  - ☐ make an overall conclusion on the most reliable source of information
  - ☐ refer to all three sources in your answer
  - ☐ interpret and/or evaluate three complex sources of information given in the question, evaluating and explaining the extent of their reliability
  - ☐ use all three sources otherwise you can only get a maximum of 5 marks
  - ☐ give evidence from the sources which supports your evaluations

The Assignment

You need to know

- that the assignment has two stages: a research stage and a production of evidence (write-up) stage

Available resources

- During the research stage, there are no restrictions on the resources you can use.
- During the write-up stage, you only have access to your research sheet (which consists of up to two sides of A4 paper).
- Your research sheet is not assessed but must be submitted to SQA with your final Assignment.

Choice of topic

- You can choose any Modern Studies topic or issue that refers to a contemporary political, social or international issue, even one that is outwith the content of Question Paper 1.
- Your topic has to be:
  - ☐ contemporary and relevant
  - ☐ a Modern Studies topic, in that it develops an understanding of the issue through using the approach of one or more of the following disciplines:
    - politics
    - sociology
    - international relations
    - economics
  - ☐ an issue that creates a range of views and possible policy options, thereby allowing a decision to be made.

Research stage

- You are allowed two sides of A4 paper as a research sheet that includes useful information and which shows evidence of research.
- Plans, knowledge, reminder or similar techniques are not allowed.
- You must refer directly to your research sheet throughout your assignment report and mention the source of your evidence, for example, author, date published, title, name of publication.

- There is no single template for a 'perfect' research sheet.
    - ☐ Lay yours out in a way that that you find useful.
    - ☐ A very carefully constructed, detailed sheet does not guarantee you will achieve high marks.
    - ☐ Similarly, a very hastily constructed, brief sheet does not mean you will achieve low marks.
- Be aware that your research sheet is not marked.
- Marks are awarded for your use of the information on your sheet, and your background knowledge.
- You must analyse and synthesise your information and combine it with your knowledge to form relevant arguments and to reach a coherent, consistent and well-supported decision.
- Avoid a research sheet which contains only a list of URLs.
    - ☐ If you do not explicitly reference a source, the marker will mark your point as 'knowledge'.
    - ☐ You may then reach the maximum of 10 marks for knowledge very quickly and lack vital analysis marks.
- Your Assignment evidence must:
    - ☐ be no more than two sides of A4 paper. There is no word limit
    - ☐ contain evidence of the actual sources used. A list of notes may not do this effectively
    - ☐ be clearly attributed (author, date published, title, name of publication)
    - ☐ contain no pre-prepared analysis or argument, however, quoting from sources is allowed
    - ☐ not contain a detailed plan with the main arguments or headings included
    - ☐ contain all the sources of information you need
    - ☐ contain no information that you intend to use as knowledge or as part of your source evaluation
    - ☐ include enough information to be useful to you but not so much as to make knowledge marks difficult to achieve

Production of evidence stage

Knowledge

- You must include points of knowledge throughout your report to frame the issue and to support your argument and analysis.

Analysis and/or synthesis

- You will gain analysis and/or synthesis marks when you use information from the sources you have collected during your research which you have included on your research sheet.
- You must make reference to, and quote from, this information when supporting an argument or policy option.

■ Large-scale copying from your research sheet, especially of pre-prepared analysis, will not gain marks.

Source evaluation
■ When evaluating sources, these must be included on your research sheet and you must make specific reference to them.

Decision
■ You will gain marks for making a clear decision or recommendation which is supported by an argument and/or specific evidence.
■ You must also consider the reasons why you discounted alternative options.

Structure
■ There is no set way to structure a report but an example of a possible layout is shown below. Remember that this is an example of how your report might be structured but such a plan must not be included in your research sheet.
■ Below is an example of a possible layout.

Example Assignment structure

Title:

Section 1: Role/remit

Section 2: Framing and background of the issue

Options
1 Recommended option
2 Alternative option 1
3 Alternative option 2

Recommendation:

Section 3: Arguments for and against recommendation

Arguments for recommendation
■
■

Arguments against recommendation
■
■

Section 4: Development of arguments for recommendation
1 First argument for recommendation
2 Second argument for recommendation
3 Third argument for recommendation

Section 5: Development of arguments against recommendation

1 First argument against recommendation

2 Second argument against recommendation

Section 6: Alternatives available

■ Alternative option 1

■ Alternative option 2

Section 7: Conclusion